Rawsome Creations

More than a Nut Milk Bag

Recipe Collection

by Brenda Hinton
with Meagan Leila Ricks

Dear First Edition Reader,

Thank you for looking at my collection of recipes.

This place in a book is where you usually find praiseful words from famous people . . . but I don't know any famous people, and anyway, this is not a book of, by, or for famous people. The simple fact that you have picked up my book and are reading these words means that you are exactly the kind of person whose feedback will be most valuable to me and future readers.

So if you read this book, and find it useful (or find ways that you think I could make it more useful) I would like to hear from you. I am especially interested to know if you had problems with any of the recipes, or if I can make the directions clearer. Also, your suggestions of variations and improvements are *very* welcome.

I hope to have a page or two of readers' thoughts for this collection's next edition. Please let me know if you like my book, and a few words about why.

I love to hear from you, so email me:

brenda@rawsomecreations.com

Again, thank you.

Brenda

More than a Nut Milk Bag

Recipe Collection

by Brenda Hinton
with Meagan Leila Ricks

Rawsome Creations
Saint Helena, California
www.rawsomecreations.com

Library of Congress Cataloging-in-Publication Data
Hinton, Brenda; Ricks, Meagan Leila
MORE THAN A NUT MILK BAG RECIPE COLLECTION
I. Title
ISBN 978-1-4782221-3-2

cover, editing, & book design: Michael Potts
CasparInstitute.org

proofreading: Mike Hinton, Sienna Potts,
Rochelle Elkan, Barbara Howard

vegetable icons: Ellie DeSilva
images on pages 92 and 94: Meagan Leila Ricks

Acknowledgements

The tapestry of my life keeps getting richer, brighter, more meaningful. Many have contributed threads to my work, and I know I will forget some; to you, I apologize. To those who lent their colors to this project, a special thank you for participating –

Michael – high school sweetheart, husband for 32 years; best fan, confidante, playmate and advisor for even longer: Your love and encouragement mean the world to me. You are my everything. Forever

Michael Potts – mentor, friend, colleague, sounding board, who translates my ideas into words that provoke change: you are the finest.

Meagan – the daughter I would have had as my own. Without your help, this collection would have been impossible. I love every minute spent with your creative inspiration and tireless energy.

Deanna – cherished sister and literary guide: your entrepreneurial entrance into global business inspires me to think big. Sisters are unique mirrors, and I treasure your reflection daily.

My parents, Larry and Edna Roesler: because your belief in me never wavers, I venture farther than I could ever imagine possible.

All my students: YOU are the reason for this book. I love knowing you are changing lives around the world. Your inspiration, encouragement, and above all, your questions shape my life. I am honored to help you see the answers to some of them.

Sienna Potts, Kiya Cote, Amy Rice, Iluh Yanti, Robin Lim, Jeff Frost, Margaret Caminsky-Shapiro, Cherie Soria , Diane Haworth, Michael Varbaek, Stacey Lapham, Susan Dobra, Linas Kesminas, Gina Hudson, Patti Searle – your inspiration, contributions, and support are more valuable than words can say.

In boundless gratitude,

Brenda
Saint Helena
July, 2012

Raw Food

Recipes

Dedication

For Michael
Forever

About this Book

You're considering nut milk and raw foods because you're ready to change your habits one step at a time, one day at a time, and slowly move up the food continuum to a more healthy lifestyle, right? Then you are in the right place, and welcome.

This book sets out to answer two questions I am often asked:

What else can I do with my
More than a Nut Milk Bag?

What can I do with the pulp after making milk?

Four ingredient story

I'd like to begin by making a confession. I don't consider myself a chef. Yes, I have a certificate which says I am a "Raw Food Chef Instructor" and I do know a thing or two about healthy foods, raw food cuisine in particular. I pay special attention to flavor balancing and the importance of making things look good and taste good while boosting energy with living ingredients that boost immune systems and give my guests that all-over glow of radiant health.

I believe with all my heart that you can learn – that's why I teach. I also know that some of the qualities that make a fabulous chef are inborn.

I didn't start out as a chef. I didn't like being in the kitchen with my Mom, and as hard as she tried through the years to help my sister and me learn how to come up with something for dinner, cooking never appealed to me. Mom had Sis and me prepare one meal a week, one night a week – we had taco salad and tuna boats a lot – so my culinary prowess did not develop early on. However, I decided at an early age that cookbooks should be easy, explicit, and complete so I could share the author's success. At the time, oh maybe 30 years ago, I never found an easy cookbook. The *Joy of Cooking* was just too big and way too complicated for my world. I remember joking with friends that I was going to write *The Four Ingredient Cook Book*. I never dreamed that I was setting into motion a set of events that would shape my life towards the present day, and the book you hold in your hands. Admittedly, these recipes have more than four ingredients – but not many more! And remembering that little girl struggling in the kitchen with obscure and incomplete recipes, I have tried hard to keep these easy, nutritious and great tasting.

This collection's several sections build from one to the next. My intention is to guide you, with easy, straight-forward recipes, through a series of successes in your kitchen. My goal: to give you skills to create authentic, tasty, healthy food choices for every day. I kept these recipes simple, but they're meant to appeal to gourmets.

Recipe Development

Here's how I approach a new recipe. The first time, I make it as the author or chef intended, along the way making notes of what to change so the recipe becomes my own. Recipe development and gradual refinement is a big part of your successful food adventure. When Meagan and I set out to assemble this collection, we worked through several iterations of each recipe, making careful notes each time of what we did and how it turned out, again noting adjustments we wanted to make for the next time. You, too, may find this conscious development process rewarding.

Our recipe format

When I cook, especially something unfamiliar, I like to read the recipe, gather all my ingredients, prepare them, sometimes read the recipe again . . . then begin to put things together. With this method in mind, complex recipes are usually broken into steps, with ingredients first, then directions for completing that step. On these complex recipes, please read through and make sure you have all the needed ingredients before launching into full preparation.

You will notice that ingredients and recipes in this collection connect in unexpected ways: soup morphs into pizza crust, juice produces crackers, nuts give milk . . . add a little of your own magic, and you will find a world of possibilities in these simple ingredients and techniques.

equipment codes

At the top of each recipe, any special tools needed will be shown with the following abbreviations:

NMB – *More than a Nut Milk Bag*
BL – High Speed Blender
FP – food processor
DH – dehydrator

knife skills & "the perfect bite"

Good knife skills are indeed important in any kitchen task but more so in raw foods. That "perfect bite" we look for in our recipes is often times achieved using equipment, such as the food processor or blender assisting us in making the bits of ingredients smooth or broken down in a particular way. Sometimes we rely on our knife to do this for us. For example, take Energy Bars (page 85): in this recipe we rely on our knife to get the dates and cashews small enough so we have that 'perfect bite' – all bits the same size as the cacao nibs: cherries, pumpkin seeds and raisins. Appreciation of this technique may take experience, so now that you know, notice how your dishes, and those made by others, achieve this perfection, or fall short. The "perfect bite" is subtle but makes a huge difference in the texture and "mouth-feel" of your finished food. The qualities that distinguish any good dish – flavor, texture, and appearance – are always important, but in raw cuisine they are supreme.

Raw Food Tools

First thing, let's look at a typical raw food kitchen's equipment list. You don't need to have everything on this list, but if you do you can make any of the recipes in this book. With that in mind, I've noted on each recipe the equipment needed to complete it; with the exception of a knife, everything is listed.

Good knives will be your new best friends you will appreciate every day. A few easy knife skills and safety techniques will serve you well as you move through the recipes and improve your culinary expertise. No need to go out and buy a fancy knife block . . . but there are a few standard knives I would recommend for your arsenal.

a good chef knife – If you're a woman with small hands, consider a Japanese knife; smaller, lighter, fits small hands beautifully, and balanced well for daily use. I love Japanese knives. There are many chef's knives on the market and I recommend you go to your local kitchen store and begin by holding them. You'll know when one feels right to you. No need to pay several hundred dollars for your first one, but I will admit, you get what you pay for. As I said above, I love the Japanese steel knives: thinner than classic German or other knives, and a good fit for my small hands. I do however have a sturdy German chef's knife for opening those tough coconuts.

a paring knife for small jobs or garnishing (should that bug bite you and you fall in love) and **a serrated knife** for those soft skin fruits and vegetables so popular in raw cuisine.

The **food processor** and **high speed blender** are the second most important pieces of equipment in the raw food kitchen. If you're new to raw fooding, these are expensive tools you may want one day, but rest assured, there are plenty of recipes in this little book that can be made without them.

I could spend pages discussing the pluses and minuses of the many brands and models, my personal opinions and how I made my decision – but I'll save that for another time.

There are two major high speed blenders to consider: the Vitamix and the Blendtec. They are very similar – in car terms, the Vitamix is the four-speed manual shift, and the Blendtec is an automatic. Many find the Blendtec easier, and that's what I chose. After awhile I graduated to a Vitamix and I love it. Each excels at specific tasks, but you can do just about anything with either. Having both, I find that I prefer my Vitamix for most things, but shift to the Blendtec for desserts like cheese-cakes, ice creams, and puddings.

Next, **a dehydrator.** You need one for some of the recipes in this book. The Excalibur nine tray model, their largest retail version, is widely used in raw food cuisine. They make smaller models but I find the nine tray is the most convenient and versatile model. The nine tray model allows you to spread out trays to every other rack within the dehydrating unit, so you have sufficient space between trays for tall things like kale chips, muffins or pizza crusts. It will also hold a large 9 x 11 ovenproof glass dish for warming foods or marinating veg-etables. The unit comes with or without a 24 hour timer; I find the timer very useful. The Excalibur folks have been making dehydrators for many years, and are raw foodists, so you *know* they're good people! Most raw food recipes, including the reci-pes in this book, are written with this model in mind. I strongly suggest buying the Paraflexx sheets. Buying everything you need in your initial purchase is cheaper than buying bits at a time.

There are some special techniques called for in managing a dehydrator – look for them in the **Techniques** section, page 26.

Here are a few things your dehydrator can be used to make:

- ❀ Crackers, cookies, chips, breads and snacks
- ❀ Sliced fruit and roll ups
- ❀ Dried herbs, spices, vegetables, nuts and seeds

In addition, you can:

- ❀ Thicken sauces
- ❀ Warm foods during the winter
- ❀ Soften coconut oil
- ❀ Marinate vegetables

Resist Consumerism!

Here's an important point: resist the urge to buy new equipment. It's often better in the beginning to borrow, or seek out slightly and gently used equipment, so you can see if you really need to spend a bundle for the newest, best and most expensive. I have gotten most of my raw food kitchen tools on-line or from other students and chefs as hand-me-downs.

My favorite "deal story" is about buying my third dehydrator. (Yes, I have three, and I know it's an obsession.) One day, on one of my many email lists, up pops a note about a brand new – "only used six times!" – Excalibur Dehydrator posted on *Craig's List*. This was the much admired nine-tray model, and included all the Paraflexx sheets, and a timer ...all for only $80! So I scored a virtually brand new unit worth close to $300 for eighty bucks.

If you put your energy out there about what you need, you're likely to be surprised. It will come to you. Trust me on this.

Tools needed for the recipes

Each recipe here has a code indicating the major equipment needed for that recipe in the upper right corner near the yield. Almost every recipe requires one or two **More than a Nut Milk Bags**.

> ## equipment codes
>
> At the top of each recipe, any special tools needed will be shown with the following abbreviations:
>
> **NMB** – *More than a Nut Milk Bag*
> **BL** – High Speed Blender
> **FP** – food processor
> **DH** – dehydrator

Other useful tools:

Spice Grinder or **Coffee Grinder** – these two are interchangeable so it's whatever you can find and add to your equipment list. I have two, one for savory spices like the herb blends that you'll find in the section on ingredients, and the other for sweet sugars like palm sugar.

Tools for dehydrating – Useful tools to have on hand for easily preparing your trays:
Offset spatulas of all sizes
Traditional spatulas
Pizza cutter
Vegetable scraper

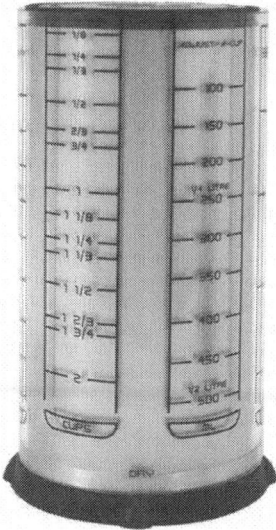

Cylindrical Measuring Cup – a very handy tool in your raw food kitchen is the adjustable measuring cup. This little gadget is one of my most favorite kitchen tools. Available in several sizes, the 1 cup version is the one I use most often. Made of plastic, it's 2 pieces with the smaller fitting inside a sleeve marked with measurements in the metric and American systems. It's helpful for a quick peek at culinary math when scaling recipes as it shows the equivalent measurements for ounces, cups, liters, milliliters, teaspoons and tablespoons. With the construction as a set of two parts, it's perfect for liquid or gooey ingredients so you can scrape every last morsel from the container. For dough (like tortillas) you can see measurements and then push the inner sleeve into the outer sleeve dispensing the exact amount of ingredient on to the trays for that uniform measure.

metrics

⅛ teaspoon		.5 ml
¼ teaspoon		1 ml
½ teaspoon		2.5 ml
1 teaspoon		5 ml
1 Tablespoon	3 teaspoons	15 ml
4 Tablespoons	¼ cup	59 ml
	⅓ cup	79 ml
	½ cup	118 ml
	1 cup	237 ml

degrees Fahrenheit / degrees Celsius

150 — 65
140 — 60
130 — 55
120 — 50
110 — 45
100 — 40

Raw Food Ingredients

Healthy Ingredients

If our goal is to raise the quality of our nutrition, then we want the best, freshest, purest ingredients. I buy organic whenever I can.

One rule for choosing ingredients: **always know your source**. Whether it is fruits, vegetables, sweeteners or simple flours, try to know who is the producer and trust them to give you the best quality you can buy. There are times when buying organic is not a choice – strawberries, the most pesticide-laden crop known, are a good example. And there are times when you may be able to consider non-organic. Please check out the Environmental Working Group website (see the Resources in the back of the book) for more information, their dirty dozen list, and up-to-date information about sourcing your food from reputable purveyors.

Personal Tastes

Recipes in this collection are meant to be guidelines, as any recipes should be. As you begin to juice and prepare recipes, you'll become more familiar with your own preferences. You may find you like more lemon or ginger in your juices than I call for; you may find you need to increase the amount of apple to make them sweeter. In the savory recipes you may find you prefer stronger garlic or salty flavor. I mean these recipes to be no more than starting places for your own creations.

About sweeteners

Choosing sweeteners is a big topic in the raw food world. Each has distinct characteristics, tastes, textures, and colors and each is used for specific reasons and recipes. I'm going to resist the temptation to discuss this here, but you can find a summary of my findings at my website.

I prefer maple syrup and have used it throughout this collection as my liquid sweetener of choice. Agave nectar can be substituted, but it is important to know your source – claims of "unprocessed" and "natural" have been found to be unreliable. I like the depth and flavor maple syrup adds to recipes, and I have developed an enjoyable relationship with a producer – we have no sugarbushes in the Napa Valley! For product sources, please check the Resources in the back of this book and online at the book's website.

Salt

I use Himalayan Crystal Salt as all the minerals are left intact. It is mined in a beautifully pristine area of the world unspoiled by environmental pollution and contamination and is at high elevations making the mineral content the finest in the world. Celtic Sea salt is another alternative.

If "local" matters to you, and you want to buy a reasonably priced domestic salt, Redmond Trading Company's Real Salt is mined from ancient oceanic salt deposits in Utah and contains a full spectrum of pelagic minerals.

Spice Blends

Ethnic foods and recipes have distinctive traditional spices that confer unique flavor profiles and aromas. As I mentioned in the opening of this book, when I started exploring the world of raw food, more than four ingredients was Intimidating, so all those spices just sent me through the roof. I'd look at things and couldn't imagine how they'd taste and what the difference all those could possibly make. Oh, did I have a lot to learn!

Since then, I have developed several spice blends – recipes in themselves, each providing a particular flavor profile – that are called for as single ingredients in the recipes in this collection.

Of course there are hundreds of possible combinations and proportions, but for our purposes and to keep this collection easy for you, these blends serve not only for the recipes in this book, but will enhance other recipes in your repertoire.

Mix these dry ingredients in small glass jars and store them in a cool, dark place and you'll have them when a recipe calls for one blend or another. In addition, they can make it easy for you in recipe development when you get adventurous in your kitchen and create something of your very own.

Asian Spice Blend
2 teaspoons cinnamon
1½ Tablespoons coriander
1½ Tablespoons turmeric
1 teaspoon clove powder
1 teaspoon paprika
2 teaspoons powdered ginger
yield: 12 teaspoons (¼ cup)
Use: ½ teaspoon in the Asian Soup recipe on page 49

Italian Spice Blend
2 Tablespoons dried basil
2 Tablespoons marjoram
1 Tablespoon garlic powder
1 Tablespoon oregano
1 Tablespoon thyme
1 Tablespoon rosemary
1 Tablespoon fennel seeds
yield: 9 Tablespoons = just over ½ cup
Use: 1 teaspoon in Italian Cracker recipe on page 63

grinding savory herbs

Best to grind savory herbs and spices right before use. Leafy herbs can be rubbed briskly between the palms of your hands to release their aromatic oils. More robust leaves and seeds call for a mortar and pestle to release their flavors. If a recipe calls for salt, adding it to the herb mix before grinding makes for an even better flavor.

Find a dealer of herbs and spices that keeps fresh and active stock, and buy small amounts of your herbs and spices in bulk. They are cheaper this way and stay fresh much longer than buying those expensive little cans and bottles that have been on the supermarket shelf for who knows how long. Plus, you're paying plenty for the packaging.

When you get the spices home mark your own jars with the date purchased. When you notice anything over six months old, throw it out. Old flavors don't add anything to recipes and their aging (oxidizing) oils can add noticeable bitterness without giving you the flavor you want.

Savory Seasoning Blend
3 Tablespoons basil
2 Tablespoons celery seed powder
1½ Tablespoons salt
2 teaspoons kelp powder
1 Tablespoon marjoram

yield: 8 tablespoons = ½ cup

Use: In Garden Blend Crackers recipe on page 68

Mexican Spice Blend
¼ cup garlic powder
1 Tablespoon ground cumin
1 Tablespoon dried basil
1 Tablespoon dried thyme
¼ cup onion powder
1½ teaspoons chili powder
1½ teaspoons dried oregano
1 teaspoon red pepper flakes

Total ¾ cup

Use: 2½ Tablespoons for Mexican Wraps on page 60

using fresh herbs

Dried herbs may usually be replaced with fresh minced herbs, however the amount will vary greatly. Typically, three parts fresh are roughly equal to one part dried.

Flavor Enhancers

tomato powder – a wonderful addition to your raw food kitchen. It adds a depth of flavor, almost a cooked flavor to any recipe. It can be purchased in bulk through your local health food store, Frontier brand. Make your own with Roma tomatoes from your garden: thin slice and dehydrate completely dry, then grind to a powder in a high speed blender or mortar and pestle. Store dried powder in your spice cabinet for use in crackers, soups, sauces, and the like. If you are unable to get tomato slices completely dry, try placing them in the freezer, then grinding them once frozen. Powder made this way should be kept frozen after grinding, as the remaining moisture can turn them to mush (or worse). You can make a really healthy and luxurious variant of this powder if you have time and a solar drier.

nutritional yeast – Make sure it's Red Star Vegetarian Support Formula fortified with vitamin B_{12}. If purchasing from the bulk section of your market, ask which supplier they stock.

mushroom powder – I save the ends of mushrooms and when I have enough for a batch, dehydrate them and then process them into a powder with a high speed blender.

spinach powder – and other seasoning powders can be made using this same technique. For more about spinach powder and an exemplary use, see page 58.

> **living foods**
>
> The power of living foods is unmistakable. Think about it: one small almond has the potential to become a huge almond tree.

Raw Food Techniques

Raw food chefs use techniques from the classical culinary world alongside more than a few special techniques of their own. Some of these are essential to these recipes and some are just decorative.

Flavor Balancing

The classic four flavors – sweet, sour (acid), salty, and bitter – are more important in raw cuisine than in conventional cooking. With a little understanding and practice you will become proficient at balancing flavors to your personal tastes and those of your guests. When something as simple as a juice includes all four flavors, it will be great every time. For instance, the Green Giant juice consists of a sweet (apple), a sour (lemon), a salty (celery), and a bitter (kale and spinach). When flavors balance, they win. When experimenting with substituting ingredients, or you find yourself missing an ingredient, think of what flavor the ingredient you're tinkering with presents – is it sweet, sour, salty, bitter? – and choose a replacement that offers similar flavors. For instance, if you don't have apple, use pear. Or vice versa. With some practice you'll find yourself adjusting recipe ideas to your taste and making up your own recipes in no time.

In addition to the classic four flavors there is pungent (strong, sharp flavors like ginger, garlic, cumin). In Green Giant Juice we add ginger to the recipe for the refreshing pungent flavor. Pungent flavors are treated judiciously in raw cuisine because these strong flavors aren't softened by cooking.

And we can't forget fat. Fat is not a flavor, but we do consider fat content of our foods carefully for two reasons. There's no doubt that fat joins sweet on most people's palette of comforting flavors. We want to keep our fats healthy (that's another book!) and we need to be careful about the amount of fat needed for flavor balance and mouth feel. Good fat in a dish – a soup, dressing, sauce, or marinade – helps different flavors play nicely together.

Alkaline vs Acidic

Every day our bodies are bombarded with acidic (oxidizing) elements everywhere we turn – our culture's technology choices, environmental noise and pollution, the toxic chemicals in our food supply. These all add up to toxic acidic overload for bodies originally designed to handle much less acidity in their daily lives. Edible plants tend naturally to be alkaline (and cooking them tends to reduce their natural alkalinity) so every opportunity we have to get raw alkaline foods into our systems gives our overloaded bodies a bit of relief.

Recycling, composting, & waste

Very little is wasted in raw food preparation. Instead, ingredients morph into new recipes, or are saved for juice. Anything left goes into the compost to enrich the garden – food for food!

Many of the recipes in this collection are designed so ingredients are utilized in more than one way. One of the questions that motivated me to assemble this recipe collection is, *What can I do with the pulp after making milk?* and we'll get to the answer in a few pages. Scraps can be saved in your fridge for the next day's juice. Since our ingredients are fresh, local, and healthy, anything we can't eat goes straight to the compost bin for the beneficial life-forms to recycle into more good food.

Storage times

Raw foods are best eaten fresh because their component parts are still alive and active. In some cases I suggest that an item can be stored, but your experience may vary. Raw foods are usually best consumed as soon as they are prepared. So leftovers need to be consumed early and often. Our best advice is 'when in doubt, throw it out.' This holds true for all foods, raw or cooked.

Soaking nuts and seeds

Sometimes, nuts and seeds need to be soaked simply to soften them. Some recipes call for nuts and seeds to be soaked for a specific amount of time. In some cases this is to allow the living seeds to sprout (germinate) and/or release enzyme inhibitors. Have you ever had a walnut that tasted extremely bitter? That taste is tannins and enzyme inhibitors in the hull. These compounds naturally protect the nuts and seeds from insects and rot until they germinate. Rain releases these inhibitors whereupon the nuts and seeds sprout (germinate) and grow into greens, plants, and trees. We accomplish the same effect by soaking them. For almonds and walnuts, this takes approximately eight hours. Softer nuts and seeds require only four to six hours. While they soak, nuts and seeds can absorb chemicals present in the water or in containers, so it's always best to use covered glass bowls or jars and filtered water.

Back to those walnuts for a minute – if you haven't tasted soaked walnuts, I invite you to give it a try. They are sweet and flavorful once the tannins and inhibitors are removed. For an even better treat, buy your almonds and walnuts in bulk, bring them home, rinse and drain them a couple of times to rinse off any harvesting, shipping and bulk-bin residue. Then soak some them for eight hours – overnight while you sleep – and in the morning put them in a dehydrator for approximately 12-24 hours until they are crispy. When they dry to crispiness, they will make a crunchy sound and crisply break when you test them. These soaked and dried nuts will store much longer than the untreated nuts from the bulk bin, and can be stored in your cupboard for months, always ready for use in recipes, for processing into flour or nut milk, for your morning breakfast, or a quick energy snack.

Dehydrating Foods

In raw and living cuisine, a dehydrator is our "slow oven." Dehydration allows us to get a "cooked" quality for crackers, snacks, cookies, cakes, and muffins that satisfies our love of crunchy textures in our diet. A dehydrator can be a wonderful addition to your kitchen (and some of these recipes call for one) but a well balanced raw food diet does not rely too heavily on dehydrated foods. Dehydrating removes water content from food – water that your digestive system promptly replaces in order to digest. So it's important to remember to drink lots of water when eating dehydrated food.

Dehydrators use low heat and air circulation to slowly remove water from food, thus drying it. You can make your own or buy one.

In raw cuisine we get our best results in the 105°–115° F (40°-46° C) range. Such low temperatures maintain the integrity of phytonutrients, anti-oxidants, and the enzymatic activity that makes raw foods radiantly nutritious. While these elements are not entirely destroyed at high temperatures – if they were you wouldn't be alive – high temperatures do degrade them, and the hotter and longer they're cooked, the greater their nutritional content is compromised.

The disagreement on the subject of the healthiness of heating food is at the very core of the raw food movement. Research continues, but there are satisfying studies, convincing experts, and anecdotal evidence enough to convince me that raw living foods, eaten in their natural state as much as possible, are better for us in the long run. With that said, dehydrated foods can be just what you need to get yourself and your loved ones over the difficult beginning stages, given our entrenched enjoyment of crunchy oily chips and sugary baked goods. Dehydrated snacks and ethnic foods (tortillas and pizza crusts like the ones included in this collection) can be winners and attract even the die-hard skeptics among your friends and families – worked for me: my initially reluctant husband is now one of my biggest raw food fans.

successful dehydrating

● When spreading dough, be sure to spread it a consistent thickness and thin if desired. This cuts down on the drying time and gives you uniform 'cooked' consistency throughout.

● Cut pieces in uniform sizes for consistent drying time.

● Times are suggestions only. Actual 'cooking' time depends on many factors –

    Climate – humid or dry?

    Time of year – cold winter? blazing summer heat?

    Location– kitchen? laundry room? outside? garage?

    And it all depends on personal taste as to the final texture of the food you are making.

● Placing a spare grid sheet on top of scored crackers helps prevent curling edges.

● Keep savory and sweet foods separated; flavors can intermingle.

● Be careful not to add another item to a dehydrator once you've begun a process. Adding 'wet' foods to something already drying can lengthen the dehydrating time and make the drying food 'wet' again.

● Using a large pizza cutter saves time when scoring. An offset spatula, veggie scraper or knife (not too sharp) can also be used.

● If foods become moist again after dehydrating – from the ambient air, refrigeration or freezer storage – put them back in the dehydrator for some time until desired texture is regained.

● Fully dehydrated foods are crispy and can be stored in an air-tight glass container for up to 3 months.

Heating temperatures – as mentioned above, raw food recipes suggest the dehydration temperature be somewhere between 105° and 115° F. Some recipes call for 125° for a short amount of time (2-3 hours), because the internal temperature of the food does not reach the "critical temp" exceeding the 105° – 115° that begins destroying nutritional values, yet it allows excess moisture to dry off immediately or helps to make the outside crunchy.

Ingredient combinations:

Some intriguing combinations prompt me to mention a little known factoid in the raw culinary world. Each dish and ingredient, in anything you make, has a distinctive flavor, texture, and appearance. In our Rawsome Creations we are striving to duplicate the flavor, texture and appearance of familiar foods, often times cooked foods, to share with our family, friends and colleagues. Everyone loves the familiarity of mashed potatoes, spaghetti and meatballs, macaroni and cheese, enchiladas and other all time favorites. All of these examples are made in the raw food world and there are many ways to convert cooked recipe components to raw

how to flip a dehydrator tray full of food

Dehydrate your recipe on the Paraflexx sheet at 115° for a limited amount of time. The Paraflexx is good for wet foods and helps them stay together until drying begins. When you can peel up the Paraflexx sheet easily and food is a bit dry to the touch, they are ready to flip. Do this by placing another dehydrator tray with grid sheet on top. Hold them together tightly and flip over. Then peel off the Paraflexx sheet leaving just your partially dried recipe on the grid sheet. This allows the air to flow sufficiently and evenly so the food dehydrates as quickly as possible. This would be the time to score your breads, crackers or bars if you have not done so. Continue dehydration until crackers are completely dry and crunchy – time will vary depending on recipe and texture desired.

versions with the culinary tricks up our sleeves. One of these is to combine like ingredients. For example, in one milk, I've combined the creamy textures of three: cashews, Brazil nuts, and hemp seeds (page 47). Each is creamy alone and has a distinctive taste. Choosing this combination ensures the creamiest milk to serve alone or incorporate into cheesecakes or ice creams. When three like ingredients are combined you achieve the texture you desire, masking the taste of single ingredients. With this combination of three and using spices and flavorings you bring your dish to its finished version with that extra Wow.

Another good example is raw mashed potatoes. By combining parsnips, cauliflower, and celery root for the creamy texture, then flavoring it to taste, you create a healthier version of this comfort food. Each component alone has a very distinctive taste, but combined and flavored it's always a winner. But that's heading toward my next recipe collection. (smile)

Blender preparation

When preparing fruits and veggies to be blended, use a *medium rough chop*, approximately ½ - 1 inch pieces to reduce wear and tear on the machinery and minimize blending time. Rough chop means uniform sized pieces not necessarily the same shape. This method is usually used when ingredients are to be blended so there is no need for precise sizes or shapes.

Liquids and high water content fruits and veggies should be placed in the blender first, down on the blades. The small pieces and high water content makes it easier for the blades to begin turning and the blender to start the blending process. In addition, this cuts down on the amount of extra water you add and shortens the blending time. You may need to blend a little first to liquefy these initial pieces to make room for additional ingredients.

This is important: don't blend any longer than is absolutely necessary to break down the food components and get the creamy textures we are looking for. The longer you blend, the more air is whipped into the mixture, often making it mousse-like. That's okay if what you want is mousse, but if not, stop before it's too late.

Water – additional water should not be necessary with the recipes here, but this will depend on the water content of all your fruits and veggies. I usually have some standing by just in case and would suggest approximately ½ cup if needed. You don't want to water down your juice; you want all those liquid nutrients with their full power and undiluted flavors.

Peeling fruits and veggies – with the exception of citrus, there's no need to peel the fruits, veggies, and greens added to your juices, provided you are buying organic. (See more about healthy ingredients on page 18.) The skins are bursting with desirable nutrients, so you're throwing away value by peeling. Flavor balancing will help adjust any additional bitterness found in the skins, and the high speed blender makes fast work of any texture you find unappealing.

Citrus - there are many methods to peel your citrus for adding to recipes and juices. Whichever way you choose, try to leave as much of the white pith as possible. Full of nutrition, this is where the bioflavonoids are located, making it the most nutritious part of the fruit.

One of the easiest ways I've found to peel citrus is to cut off the top and bottom first – just a little, enough to give a stable working surface; you don't want to waste too much. With the bottom resting on your cutting board, using a sharp knife, begin at the top, cutting through the skin but leaving some of the pith, let your knife curve around the contour of the citrus and end up on the cutting board, removing a piece of the outer peel. Work your way around the citrus, removing small pieces of the peel with each turn. Citrus peel is usually placed in the garbage as it doesn't compost well.

More than a Nut Milk Bag Recipe Collection

Pulp – recipes in this collection use pulp left behind when making milks and juices. The pulp left when blending juice ingredients usually has greater moisture content than the nut milk pulp. This wet pulp can be used in cracker recipes with the addition of soaked flax seeds, spices, and perhaps sweeteners, but the dehydration time will be longer due to the moisture content. Additionally, when making crackers with this pulp, I suggest you set the dehydrator at 125° for up to 2 hours, then drop the temperature to 105°. This will allow the high moisture to evaporate and create a safer environment for the long slow dehydration process to keep it "raw". This high temperature for a short period of time does not reach 'critical temp' and degrade the nutrients in the raw ingredients.

Pulp can usually be refrigerated for three days or frozen for up to one month.

Seeds and stems – when chopping your fruits, greens or veggies for juice recipes, there is no need to discard the small seeds nor de-stem the greens. There is nutrition in these little gems and the blender will make quick work of incorporating them into your juice before straining.

You were probably told not to eat apple seeds, because they are poison. Yes, they do contain a tiny bit of cyanide (not arsenic as many believe) to keep the bugs from eating them, but honestly, there's not enough to cause harm to humans in the amounts contained in juice. The same goes for grape, watermelon, and even flax seeds. Most fruits contain components called *alkaloids* – naturally occurring chemical compounds found primarily in plants. These are also part of Mother Nature's protective system. To avoid complete extinction in the natural world, many plants have equipped themselves with toxic substances, in small amounts, so hungry wandering critters will experience a bitter taste and steer clear. Instead, the critters move on to sweeter morsels, leaving behind enough seedlings, sprouts, or sprigs to grow again. Ahh, the wonders of nature.

Enough about tools and techniques. Let's get to the recipes!

This little collection is collaborative, and as soon as you start working with these recipes, you're likely to learn things I don't know . . . so **stay in touch** through the book's website**.** Be sure to let me know what miraculous things happen in your recipe creations. I'd love to share your enjoyment.

children in the kitchen

Most raw food recipes are child-friendly. Not only do the young ones get to help with their hands in the food (we all love to eat with our hands – look how popular tacos, burritos, pizza are). Share kitchen time with your children and their friends to make food preparation familiar, fun, and less work for everyone. When children see the process from the beginning they learn to prefer healthy options because they had a stake in creating them.

Beverages

For many of my students, the road to raw starts with simple-to-make healthy juices and some light green tea recipes like the ones in this section. Juices are packed full of nutrition and goodness. They preserve the concentrated vitamins and minerals contained in vegetables and fruit, and present them to your body in a way that allows rapid absorption – from the garden into your cells in less than 25 minutes. *That's* fast food!

Juicing has long been used as a method for rapid healing at clinics and health spas in almost every culture. Experts like Max Gerson and Norman Walker champion detoxification and and demonstrate miraculous healings. Quality juicers are ideal for extracting juices, but machines constructed especially for this task are expensive. I love mine and use it almost daily ...but I started experimenting with juices using a humble household blender. If you have a juicer, use it instead of a blender, but if you don't, I want to encourage you to try juicing. It's a great way to start evolving toward a raw living food diet.

about blending and high speed blenders

Any of the recipes in this collection which use a high speed blender can be made in a standard home blender. Use 'old faithful' until it begs to be replaced, then consider stepping up to a high speed blender like a Vitamix or Blendtec. These professional quality blenders make quick work of fruits, veggies and just about anything else you put in. They quickly change rough ingredients into creamy soups, juices, sauces, desserts, and smoothies.

Carrot Ginger Juice

Carrots and Ginger – a winning combination in my book. I love the sweetness of carrots combined with that classic zing of ginger in juices, soups, and sauces. Carrots are high in beta-carotene (a powerful anti-oxidant), and Vitamin A (an immune system regulator). Carrots are full of carotenoids, which are red, yellow, or orange-colored compounds found in many edible plants. Studies indicate that a diet high in carotenoids can lead to a reduced risk of cancers, so carrots are one of Earth's healthiest foods. Combined with ginger, a powerful anti-inflammatory, anti-microbial, and anti-bacterial, this juice is a powerhouse full of goodness any time of day.

Yields 16 oz juice, approximately 1 cup pulp   **NMB BL**

Ingredients:
- ½ **medium lemon** peeled
- **4 large celery stalks**
- **1 medium apple**
- **2 large carrots**
- **Thumb-sized knob of ginger**
- **optional: ½ cup water**

Directions:

Rough chop (see Glossary) the lemon, celery, apple, and carrots into medium pieces (approximately 1 inch). Place all ingredients in high speed blender in the order they are listed. Blend smooth (about 1 minute cycle). The plunger may be needed to get things started. Strain blended mixture through a ***More than a Nut Milk Bag***, easily 'milking' the pulp and catching the juice in a bowl or pitcher. Serve immediately. Save the pulp for use in other recipes. (Example: Carrot Ginger Crackers on page 61)

Pulp can be refrigerated for 3 days or frozen for up to 1 month.

Green Giant Juice

Kale is King – one of the healthiest leafy greens on the planet and one of my favorites. It comes in many varieties – Dinosaur, Curly, Russian, Ornamental, to name a few – and every one is packed with nutrition: calcium, fiber, iron, beta-carotene (a powerful anti-oxidant) and Vitamins A, C and K. Kale is a powerful, versatile green energy that enriches smoothies, salads, and green juices.

Yield: 16 oz of juice / approximately 1 cup pulp   **NMB BL**

Ingredients:
- ½ **cup water**
- 1 **medium lemon** peeled
- 2 **large celery stalks**
- ½ **medium apple**
- ¼ **cup parsley** packed measure (4-5 sprigs)
- 1 **cup spinach** packed measure (1 large handful)
- **Thumb-sized knob of ginger**
- 1 **cup kale leaves** packed measure (3 large sized leaves)

Directions:

Rough chop (see Glossary) the lemon, celery, and apple into medium pieces (approximately 1 inch). Place all ingredients in high speed blender in the order they are listed. Blend smooth (about 1 minute cycle). The plunger may be needed to get things started. Strain blended mixture through a ***More than a Nut Milk Bag***, easily 'milking' the pulp and catching the juice in a bowl or pitcher. Serve immediately. Save the pulp for use in other recipes. (Examples: Spinach Wraps, page 58 or Garden Blend Crackers, page 68)

Additions

Add 1 cucumber, rough chopped for another level of flavor and nutrition.

Detox Green Juice

Dandelion, parsley, cilantro and burdock root – powerful detoxifying foods! I can hear the groans now as you think of these bitter greens and roots and how you couldn't possibly get them to taste good. By adding the sweetness of apple, the tartness of lemon, and the fresh taste of cucumber, you balance the bitter tastes and produce a juice full of flavor and healing qualities.

In addition to being full of vitamins and minerals, experts tell us that this combination greatly enhances the body's ability to release toxins, purify the blood, remove heavy metals, detoxify, and cleanse the liver, and stimulate the digestive organs. With its powerful natural cleansing agents, this juice is a great way to begin your day, add to your cleansing regimen, or enjoy anytime.

Dandelion greens – very high in calcium, iron and Vitamins A and C, help detoxify, and cleanse the liver.

Parsley and Cilantro – natural chelators that help remove heavy metals from the body.

Burdock Root purifies the blood, flushes toxins, and stimulates the digestive organs.

Burdock Root

I first learned about burdock root during my active cancer journey. Burdock root is one of the main components of the famous Essiac Tea created by Rene Caisse (Essiac spelled backwards) in the 1920's. Her tea formula has been used by thousands worldwide as a component in natural cancer fighting therapies. The herbal combinations in this tea build the immune system, detoxify, and are said to kill cancer cells. With testimonials from across the world and personal experience of the healing powers of foods I include burdock root in my juices as often as I can.

More than a Nut Milk Bag Recipe Collection

Ingredients:
- 1 large cucumber
- 1 medium apple rough chopped
- 1½ medium lemons peeled and rough chopped
- ½ cup dandelion greens (packed measure) about a third of a bunch
- ½ bunch kale (3-4 cups packed measure)
- 1 cup parsley (about a quarter bunch or 8-9 sprigs packed measure)
- ½ cup cilantro (about 8-9 sprigs packed measure)
- 2-inch long ½ inch diameter knob of burdock root

Directions:

Rough chop (see Glossary) the apple and lemons into medium pieces (approximately 1 inch). Place all ingredients in high speed blender in the order they are listed. Blend smooth (about 1 minute cycle). The plunger may be needed to get things started. Strain blended mixture through a ***More than a Nut Milk Bag***, easily 'milking' the pulp and catching the juice in a bowl or pitcher. Serve immediately. Save the pulp for use in other recipes. (Example: Garden Blend Crackers, page 68)

Additions:

If you are feeling a bit under the weather or sense a cold or flu coming on, add a couple of cloves of garlic or a warming ingredient such as ginger or cayenne to this juice. This will give your immune system just the kick you need to fight off the baddies and open up your sinuses.

two bags make clearer juice!

Strain your mixture through two nested ***More than a Nut Milk Bags*** for clearer juice.

Electro-Lemonade

As a recreational runner I'm always looking for something to carry with me for that quick refreshment out on a long run. Coconut water has long been one of my favorites; the closest thing to human blood plasma, it refreshes the cells quickly and energizes me to keep going. This quick easy "lemon aide" is for me a close second, helping me over the hump for years. Packed with nutrition and electrolytes, it's great for long runs, to serve visitors on hot summer days or for a quick tangy pick-up when your energy dips.

A tip of the raw food *toque blanc* to Chefs Diane Haworth and Michael Varbaek for this life-saving recipe.

Yield: 4-5 cups with pulp   **NMB BL**

Ingredients:
   6 cups red seedless grapes
   ½ lemon with the rind
   ½ to 1 inch slice of ginger

Directions:
   Combine all ingredients in the order listed in a high speed blender and blend on high for 1 minute.

   Enjoy as is or strain through a **More than a Nut Milk Bag**.

---

equipment codes

At the top of each recipe, any special tools needed will be shown with the following abbreviations:

NMB – *More than a Nut Milk Bag*

BL – High Speed Blender

FP – food processor

DH – dehydrator

Health Benefits:

High in the ABC vitamins, grapes are stocked with electrolytes, especially potassium. They are a low glycemic fruit, contain resveratrol (especially red grapes), and powerhouse phytonutrients in the skins (also in seeds and flesh but not as much). High in anti-oxidants and iron, grapes have been shown to increase longevity, and can help lower cholesterol and retard the growth of skin cancer. Wow, now there's some powerful fruit!

Lemons are alkalizing to the body and great liver tonifiers. Ginger, a warming rhizome, is great for circulation and a powerful anti-inflammatory. With all this going on, no wonder I like Electro-Lemonade for those long runs. Energy, nutrients, and pain relief – gotta love it !

Star Anise Green Tea Nectar

When I began weaning myself from caffeine, I read a lot about the healthy benefits of green tea. I found it bitter at first, and a challenge to get used to, but now I love it and often begin my day with a cup. Enjoying green tea hot or cold can add much needed antioxidants that are reputed to reduce the risks of developing many types of cancer.

Here's my version of green tea lemonade with an extra surprise of star anise, a popular spice in Indian cuisine that reputedly has antiviral, antibacterial, and antifungal properties, provides the health benefits of anti-oxidants and phytonutrients, and assists with digestive health. All in all, a powerful spice that enlivens this nectar. Star anise is said by many to have magical spiritual qualities that help us experience our connection to the divine. Why not give it a try?

Yield: 7 cups   **NMB BL**

Ingredients
- **6 cups brewed green tea** (see directions)
- **¼ cup lime juice** (about 4 limes)
- **¾ cup orange juice** (about 3 oranges)
- **¼ – ½ cup agave nectar** (start with ¼ cup, sweeten as desired)
- **5 star anise pods**
- **5 cinnamon sticks**

Green Tea & Lycopene

Choosing to regularly eat lycopene-rich foods, such as pink grapefruit, and drink green tea may greatly reduce a man's risk of developing prostate cancer."
– the *Asia Pacific Journal of Clinical Nutrition*,
Jian L, Lee AH, et al.

Directions:

If it's sunny and you're not in a hurry, place 6 cups of water and 3 teaspoons of your favorite green tea in a **More than a Nut Milk Bag** into a large jar or container and set it outside for a sun tea infusion. Otherwise, bring the water *almost* to a boil and pour over the bag in the container. Steep for desired length of time, remove (and save) tea leaves and set tea aside to cool. (See Glossary for more about green tea.)

To make lime and orange juice: Using a knife, remove outer peel from the limes and oranges. Leaving pith is fine as it contains many of the nutrients. Rough chop citrus once peeled and place in a high speed blender. Blend until smooth, or for about 20 seconds. Strain blended mixture through a **More than a Nut Milk Bag** and catch resulting juice in a bowl or pitcher. Set aside to add to tea once brewed.

Add citrus juice to the brewed green tea along with the agave nectar, anise pods, and cinnamon sticks. (Note: it is easier to add agave nectar when the mixture is still warm.)

Place the jar in a warm area overnight or about eight hours to allow the flavors to marry. Strain out the star anise pods and cinnamon sticks using a **More than a Nut Milk Bag**. Serve at room temperature or chilled.

May be stored in the refrigerator for up to one week.

Green Tea

"Taken altogether, the evidence certainly suggests that incorporating at least a few cups of green tea every day will positively affect your health. It's not going to cure anything and it shouldn't be consumed as a drug, but it can complement the rest of the diet."

– Diane McKay, PhD
Tufts University scientist
who studies antioxidants

Grapefruit Juice Cooler

Inexpensive and available all year, red grapes and grapefruit are rich sources of essential vitamins and nutrients. Low on the glycemic index and packed with antioxidants, both play a role in longevity, are rich in phytonutrients (grapes contain resveratrol and red grapefruit are high in lycopene) and high in Vitamin C. Combined, the sweet and sour of these fruits balance each other beautifully for a classic taste combination.

Yield: 16 oz of juice and about 1 cup of pulp   **NMB BL**

Ingredients:
   1½ cups red seedless grapes (about 45-50 grapes)
   ½ large grapefruit peeled and rough chopped
   1 large stalk of celery
   2 medium apples rough chopped
   ½ cup parsley packed measure (about 8-10 sprigs)
   1 cup spinach packed measure (1 large handful)

Directions:
   Rough chop the grapefruit, celery, and apple into medium pieces (approximately 1 inch). Place all ingredients in high speed blender in the order they are listed. Blend smooth (about 1 minute cycle). The plunger may be needed to get things started. You might need to blend a little before adding the 'greens' to get the water content up as needed to ensure all the ingredients blend well. Strain blended mixture through a ***More than a Nut Milk Bag***, gently 'milking' the pulp and catching the juice in a bowl or pitcher. Serve immediately because Vitamin C starts to degrade the instant it hits the air. Save the pulp for use in other recipes.

Addition:
   Add a thumb-sized piece of ginger for that extra zing.

Milks and Creams

Making milks and creams is easy. The difference between the two is simply the amount of water you add to your soaked nuts: less water, the thicker the mixture; more water, the thinner. The ratio I use is 1:3 for milk and 1:1 for heavy cream. The resulting liquid, once strained through the **More than a Nut Milk Bag**, is thicker or thinner depending on this ratio.

If milk is wanted, use one cup soaked almonds to three cups water. If something a little thicker is needed, such as a half and half, the ratio would be 1:2 (one cup almonds to two cups water). If heavy cream is called for, the ratio is 1:1 or 1:1¼. Same goes for coconut milk and cream (but these don't need to be strained).

---

equipment codes

At the top of each recipe, any special tools needed will be shown with the following abbreviations:

NMB – **More than a Nut Milk Bag**

BL – High Speed Blender

FP – food processor

DH – dehydrator

---

blender management

When making nut milks a simple technique comes in handy – place the nuts in the blender first down by the blades, measure your water but add only enough to the blender to cover the nuts. Begin blending for a short time while the nuts are broken into small bits (about 15 seconds). Then add the remaining water and continue blending until well incorporated and nuts are completely broken down. Beginning the blending process with only a small amount of water keeps the nuts down near the blades so they are broken quickly and uniformly. If you add all of the water to the nuts when you begin the blending process the nuts get an exciting ride but only hit the blades occasionally, so your blending time is much longer, and this introduces more air into the mixture, making it less creamy. Less blending invariably means a more flavorful, better textured product.

pre-soaking

Most nut milks require soaking the nuts or seeds 4-8 hours. This not only makes them soft but releases their enzyme inhibitors. (See Glossary and page 25.) Neither cashews nor Brazil nuts will sprout or release enzyme inhibitors when soaked, so if you are using their creamy luscious milk, you needn't bother to soak them. If making a cream, they can be soaked 4-6 hours to soften them just a bit before blending.

If you are in a rush or forgot to soak the nuts originally chosen, remember if you always have cashews, Brazil nuts or hemp seeds on hand, you can have luscious milk in no time.

Almond Milk

Almond milk is one of the most popular nut milks and the reason I began the **More than a Nut Milk Bag** project. Almonds are called the Queen of Nuts (although the almond is a seed, not a nut. Those Royals!) because they are high in protein, fiber, calcium, magnesium, and potassium and are said to reduce cholesterol levels, prevent osteoporosis, and regulate blood pressure. Extremely alkalizing to the body, almonds are worthy additions to your daily *food as medicine* regime.

Yields about 2½ cups   **NMB BL**

Ingredients:
   1 cup almonds soaked 6-8 hours in cool water
   3 cups water

Directions
   Rinse and drain soaked almonds thoroughly. Place drained almonds in a high speed blender along with enough water to cover the nuts. Blend until smooth, about one minute, then add remaining water and blend briefly. Strain blended mixture through **More than a Nut Milk Bag** and catch resulting milk in a bowl or pitcher.

---

two bags make smoother milks & creams

One or two **More than a Nut Milk Bags** can be used for milk and cream recipes. One is sufficient, but adding a second one nestled inside the first in your pitcher creates an extra filter for catching smaller grains and yielding a very fine cream for desserts such as whipped almond cream topping.

Almond Cream

Yields about 1¼ cups   **NMB BL**

Ingredients:
   1 cup almonds soaked 6-8 hours in cool water
   1¼ cups water (maybe a little more depending on personal
      preference)

Directions:

   Rinse and drain soaked almonds thoroughly. Place drained almonds in a high speed blender along with water. (See notes below.) Blend until smooth or about one minute. Strain blended mixture through ***More than a Nut Milk Bag*** and catch resulting milk in a bowl or pitcher.

storing milk and pulp

   Most milks can be stored in refrigerator 3-5 days in sealed glass container.
   Pulp can be frozen for storage and saved for future recipe use. Freeze in small measured amounts so you only thaw what you need for future recipes.

100% hemp seed milk

   Unlike other nut milks, 100% Hemp Seed Milk does not require straining after blending. So for a quick, nutritious, creamy seed milk, blend hemp seeds and water until creamy and serve. High in protein, EFA's, phytonutrients and containing all nine of the essential amino acids, hemp seeds are a storehouse of nutritional benefits. Add them to your day by making milk, sprinkling them on a salad, or adding them to your shake or smoothie.

Cashew-Brazil-Hempseed Milk

This combination of three softer nutritionally powerful seeds makes a creamy luscious milk or cream for desserts, smoothies or simply over granola. Called nuts, Brazils and cashews are actually seeds and they do not contain the enzyme inhibitors common to nuts. (See Glossary for more about this.)

Brazil nut trees, one of the tallest in the tropical rainforest, have a life span of 500-700 years. Now that's healthy! Brazil nuts (seeds) are easy to digest, high in good fats, and exceptionally high in selenium – in fact, the highest natural content of this mineral. One nut a day satisfies your body's need for this indispensable mineral. Cashews, widely documented to increase heart health, are high in magnesium and help balance calcium, thus regulating bone health in the body. As an added benefit, cashews are lower in fat than most other nuts. Both hemp seeds and Brazil nuts are packed with protein.

Yields 2½ - 3 cups **NMB BL**

Ingredients:
  ¼ cup cashews
  ¼ cup Brazil nuts
  ¼ cup hemp seeds
  2 cups water

Directions:
  Place nuts and hemp seeds into a high speed blender along with the water.

  Blend ingredients smooth (about 30 seconds – 1 minute). Place blended mixture into two **More than a Nut Milk Bags** nestled one inside the other. Strain resulting nut milk, catching the liquid in a bowl or pitcher. Note: this milk recipe produces less pulp than almond milk. Cashews and hemp seeds do not release pulp or skins, and the Brazil nuts release only a little.

Soups

I'm a true lover of soups, salads, crackers and just about anything with lots of texture. In the wintertime, everyone always asks me "What do you do to stay raw? Don't you crave hot foods?" I love a good warm soup and during the winter I enjoy them several nights a week. I have collected several favorites here.

In raw cuisine we play with texture, flavor, and appearance. Over-processed foods can easily become soft and mushy. By thoughtfully staging carefully prepared ingredients, the original nature of the raw living food is preserved, and the soup is more exciting.

To make your soups warm, heat them on the stovetop using a thermometer or your finger. I figure if it's not too hot for my finger, it's not over 115°.

When making soup, even traditional recipes, you seldom need to boil the soup. How many times have you done this and then waited for it to cool enough to be eaten? Raw foodists point out that all that heat wipes out valuable nutrients and wastes energy! If you remember to heat soup only to a warm temperature, you can enjoy all the great taste without burning your tongue, while preserving the nutrients, enzymes, anti-oxidants, phytochemicals, and reducing your carbon footprint!

High-speed blenders can blend soup until it's too hot. Mind the temperature while blending, as these blenders can have your ingredients steaming before you know it.

soup skills

Raw soups are great places to sharpen your knife skills, because your beautifully cut ingredients are show-cased in the dish. Here's a little culinary secret – you can buy julienne cut peelers and mandolins, tools that shorten your prep time dramatically.

Asian-Thai Inspired Soup

This Thai inspired soup has the classic flavors of coconut, chilis, lemon grass and Asian spices. The broth is easy to prepare and you'll have the opportunity to sharpen your knife skills as you perfect the classic 'julienne' cut on several different types of vegetables which add that 'noodle' quality to the soup.

Yields: 6 cups   **NMB BL**

Broth Ingredients:
- **3-4 large stalks celery** rough chopped (about 3 cups)
- **1 large cucumber** peeled and rough chopped (about 4 cups)
- **2½ cups coconut water** (the water from 2 young Thai coconuts)
- **3 Tablespoons lemon juice**
- **2 Tablespoons fresh lemon grass** chopped (about one small lemon grass stalk)

Broth Directions:
Add ingredients to high speed blender and blend until smooth, about 1 minute. Place **More than a Nut Milk Bags** over a large pitcher and strain blended mixture through one or two bags. Return broth to the blender once strained.

Soup Ingredients:
- **2 Tablespoons white miso**
- **½ teaspoon Asian Spice Blend** (page 20)

Add to the broth and blend until spices are fully incorporated.

recipe continues on the next page

Noodle Ingredients:

- **1 cup mung bean sprouts**
- **1 cup kelp noodles** rinsed and soaked to soften – cut into 1½ to 2 inch long pieces
- **1 avocado** julienned (cut in thin strips)
- **½ cup carrot** julienned in 1" long pieces (use a julienne peeler)
- **½ cup baby bok choy** thinly sliced strips cut into 1-inch long pieces
- **½ cup shiitake mushrooms** thinly sliced
- **¼ cup snow peas** thinly sliced strips
- **¼ cup hijiki** soaked to soften, strain before adding to soup

Noodle Directions

Prepare vegetables and hand fold into the soup base. Serve chilled, or at room temperature.

Options:

Coconut meat can also be used for noodles. Thinly slice (julienne) the meat of one young Thai coconut and cut strips into one inch pieces. Fold these in with the other 'noodles.'

---

spicier soup

Add **1 Thai chili pod** cut in half and de-seeded or **⅛ teaspoon cayenne**. To prepare Thai chili-pod: Submerge chili pod into the soup mixture for 5-10 minutes. Promptly remove as the chili is very hot and will continue to carry its spice over into the mixture the longer it sits.

---

smidgen & pinch

Smidgen and pinch are actual culinary terms. They may sound almost insignificant, but small amounts of these usually potent ingredients make all the difference in a recipe. These terms together may sound like a law firm, but they usually apply to pungent spices such as ginger, paprika, and cloves.

Minestrone

This classic Italian favorite will again challenge your knife skills, but the result is your reward. Enjoy it with a large salad or by itself as a soup with attitude. Be imaginative about ingredients: basically just salad ingredients in a different form.

Yields 6 cups   **NMB BL**

3 large Roma tomatoes rough chopped
2 cups orange juice (about 2 medium oranges)

Peel the oranges, cutting away the pith and rind. Rough chop peeled oranges and tomatoes and place in a high speed blender. Blend smooth, or for about 30-40 seconds. Strain blended mixture through a ***More than a Nut Milk Bag*** and catch resulting juice in a mixing bowl. This produces about four cups of juice. Set aside.

Whisk in:
1 teaspoon salt
1 teaspoon coriander
1 teaspoon cumin
1 teaspoon onion powder
4 teaspoons tomato powder

Fold in the following vegetables:
½ **cup zucchini** finely diced
½ **cup Roma tomato** finely diced
½ **cup carrot** finely diced
½ **cup celery** finely diced
½ **cup corn kernels**
½ **cup peas**
½ **cup broccoli florets** finely cut (optional)

Serve chilled or at room temperature.

heating soup

To heat these soups during the summer (or anytime) I put the soup mixture in a pot on the stove and using a thermometer or my finger I continually check the temperature to be sure the soup stays below 115°.

Sweet Corn Chowder

One of my husband's favorite raw soups. Corn Chowder has become a staple in our home. Serve any time of year at room temperature or warmed on chilly winter nights. During the summer months when sweet corn is plentiful I use fresh, but the organic frozen sweet corn available at most healthy stores is a great substitute and available year round. If there happens to be any soup left over, it can easily be made into corn tortillas for chips or taco shells (two following recipes).

Yields 6 cups   **BL**

Ingredients:

6 cups of sweet corn kernels divided into two equal
portions (about six ears of fresh corn or two 16 ounce
bags frozen sweet corn)

1 cup almond milk (see recipe page 45)

2 Tablespoons lime juice

2 teaspoons white miso

1 teaspoon fresh garlic (1 large clove)

1 Tablespoon Red Star nutritional yeast

1 teaspoon cumin

⅛ teaspoon jalapeno chili powder

1 teaspoon salt

¼ cup minced red onion

Directions:

In a high speed blender, place 3 cups – half the amount of corn – almond milk, lime juice, white miso, garlic, nutritional yeast, cumin, jalapeno powder, and salt. Blend until mixture is smooth. Transfer mixture to a mixing bowl and gently fold in the remaining 3 cups of corn and the minced onion. Garnish with chili flakes and freshly ground pepper. Serve chilled or at room temperature.

May be stored in an air tight glass container in the refrigerator for up to one week, or frozen for up to 2 months.

Corn Tortillas

With leftover **Corn Chowder** or for a whole batch of tortillas or taco shells, here's an easy recipe for sweet corn tortillas.

Yields 20-25 6" tortillas or 100+ chips depending on size

BL DH

Ingredients:

Before removing Corn Chowder mixture (page 52) from the high speed blender add the following while the blades are turning slowly:

¼ **cup golden flax seeds** ground separately in a coffee or spice grinder

1 **Tablespoon psyllium powder**

Directions:

Pulse or blend until well incorporated throughout.

Ready six dehydrator trays with grid and Paraflexx sheets. Using a Paraflexx lined dehydrator tray and template (see page 55) as a guide, spread a generous ¼ cup of the mixture for each tortilla round. Using a small offset spatula, spread the mixture flat and smooth so that it fills out the entire round evenly. If not using template: use 1/4 cup measure of mixture for each 6 inch tortilla and spread evenly (about ⅛ inch thick) forming 4 circles for wraps on each Paraflexx sheet. Repeat until all the mixture is distributed. Dehydrate at 115° Fahrenheit for 7-8 hours.

recipe continues on the next page

psyllium powder

Psyllium powder is used as a thickener for these tortillas. There are many ingredients used in raw food cuisine as thickeners and binders. Psyllium adds a pliable quality to the tortillas so they will bend for tacos. With additional psyllium (approximately 3 tablespoons total) these tortillas should be pliable enough to roll for burritos or enchiladas.

Place a second dehydrator tray (with grid sheet only, no Paraflexx) on top of the partially dried tray of tortillas and flip the entire assembly over. Peel off Paraflexx sheet, leaving tortilla batter on the grid sheet only. Continue drying until desired consistency is reached – dry yet pliable.

Tortillas (if dried completely) can be stored in the cupboard for months, or in the refrigerator or freezer for up to two months.

spreading dough

Spreading dough on dehydrator trays is a challenge the first few times. Practice makes perfect – many find this time very meditative and for me it's often that special Zen like moment in my kitchen. Until you've mastered it, here are some tips for the process I've found most helpful:

The easiest way to explain it:

First be sure you have plenty of counter space (no clutter nearby) so you can easily turn the whole tray as you spread.

A small offset spatula is best for this task. Hold the spatula as light as air and begin spreading from the middle outwards.

Continue spreading softly and smoothly until you attain the desired size and thickness.

You can use the back of the spatula to help with rounding the edges and giving your dough the exact shape you are looking for.

Make sure the dough is even across the entire surface as this helps reduce dehydrator drying time.

Tortilla Chips

Make the Corn Chowder recipe (page 52) adding the golden flax seed meal and psyllium powder as described in the Corn Tortillas recipe (page 53). Prepare six dehydrator trays. Once ingredients are totally blended, use a 2-cup measure to distribute four generous quarter cups of batter onto each dehydrator trays. Dehydrate until completely crispy.

tortilla tips

To prevent the edges from curling when drying tortillas, wraps or crepes place a dehydrator grid sheet only on top of your tray once it's flipped.

If tortillas should take on a bit of moisture from the environment (cupboard, refrigerator, or freezer) place them back into the dehydrator and dry them until they reach their former consistency.

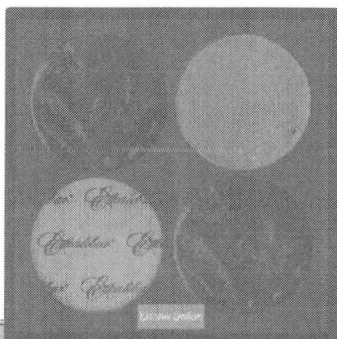

useful template

A tool that chefs find especially helpful: a food grade acrylic **TEMPLATE** that fits directly over the Excalibur dehydrator trays to help create four uniform 6 inch tortillas, wraps, or crêpes quickly and easily. Easy to wash and store, bring it out for production mode, teaching, or just for extra help making things round. A *Rawsome Creations* exclusive, available only at RawsomeCreations.com !

Wraps, Crackers, and Bread

"Crunch" is something that can easily go missing in an all-living foods diet, but with some ingenuity, an innovative ingredient (bloomed quinoa), liberal helpings of herbs and spices, and the magic of a dehydrator, we can easily get crunch back. As we saw in the last chapter (where corn chowder morphed into tortillas and chips, page 53), the possibilities are limited only by our imagination.

Bread is another food that many who are evolving their diets away from gluten and toward raw find hard to give up. I love a good scone or muffin with my cheery morning cup of tea, so I am always looking for ways to recreate these simple joys using raw food techniques and ingredients. Using left-over pulp, dried fruits, and other raw cuisine techniques, I have developed some healthy substitutes that should satisfy the most stubborn bread-lover:

bloomed quinoa

A big Thank You to my creative partner Meagan for this. She's been playing in the kitchen for some time to perfect this new culinary technique and finding all sorts of ways to use it. Bloomed Quinoa (BQ) is not technically raw because it's slowly dehydrated at 145°, but my body loves it and I've begun including it whenever I can. Rinsed thoroughly, BQ will last in the refrigerator for up to one week so it can be available for quick salads or inclusion in a favorite recipe that calls for something extra. Adding a bit of texture if not completely blended and bumping up the protein, BQ adds no noticeable flavor and so becomes a healthful silent partner in whatever dish you make.

Bloomed Quinoa

Many of us love grains – oatmeal in the morning, rice with Mexican or Asian foods, and that ever-present wheat found in our favorite breads and pastries. In the raw food world certain grains are still a part of our cuisine, but we treat them differently, using culinary legerdemain to keep them as healthy and close to their natural state as possible. A raw version of oatmeal is one of my family's favorites in the morning. Bloomed wild rice, zucchini, cauliflower, or cabbage rice can be used in Mexican or Asian dishes. And with a little magic in the kitchen, some breads, scones, or muffins can be made with what we are calling **bloomed quinoa**. Ok, so it's not totally raw as its temperature is raised to 145° for the blooming process, but it's closer to a raw version than the boiled counterpart, and it's full of protein. My body loves it, and that's always my gauge.

Yield: approximately 7 cups

Ingredients
   1½ cups quinoa
   6 cups water

Directions:

Place quinoa and water in a sealable half gallon or full gallon glass jar. Seal securely and place in the dehydrator on 145° for 24-48 hours until quinoa reaches desired softness.

Once done, drain quinoa through a **More than a Nut Milk Bag**. Rinse and drain quinoa thoroughly until water runs clear – about 4-6 rinse cycles.

Stored in an air tight glass jar, bloomed quinoa will keep in the refrigerator for up to two weeks *if rinsed and drained thoroughly*. It's wonderful to have around for toppings on salads, inside tacos, a sweet tapioca type dessert by adding some raisins and sweetener or make some into muffins, breads or scones. (see recipes on pages 58, 60, 68)

Spinach Wraps

I don't remember when wraps became popular but they've added another dimension to hand held culinary delights that I've grown to love. Using wraps to change up your menu is an easy way to bring ethnic tradition to simple veggies. Included in these recipes is the use of Bloomed Quinoa, a new raw food culinary technique. The addition of the quinoa is completely optional, the wraps will still taste great without it, but its addition brings a depth of texture and bumps up the protein to a whole new level. In addition, the use of culinary powders (spinach and tomato) bring the flavor quotient up and I hope you agree, these are worth inclusion in your weekly menu planning.

Yield: about 3¼ cups of mixture or about 10-13 (6) inch wraps

BL DH

2 batches of Green Giant Juice pulp (page 35)
½ cup olive oil
1 cup coconut meat
2 Tablespoons Irish moss paste or equivalent amount kelp noodles (see tip on page 92)
2½ cups spinach packed measure
2 cups Bloomed Quinoa (page 57)
2 Tablespoons spinach powder (page 22)
½ teaspoon onion powder
¼ teaspoon garlic powder
½ teaspoon ground pepper
½ teaspoon salt
¼-½ cup of water to blend

Blend all ingredients in a high speed blender *in the order listed*, utilizing as much water needed to blend.

Using a Paraflexx lined dehydrator tray and template as a guide, spread a heaping ¼ cup mixture for each wrap round.

Using a small offset spatula, spread the mixture flat and smooth so that it fills out the entire round evenly.

If not using a template: use ¼ cup measure of mixture for each 6 inch tortilla and spread evenly (about ⅛ inch thick) forming 4 circles for wraps on each Paraflexx sheet.

Repeat until all the mixture is distributed.

Place trays in the dehydrator and dehydrate at 115° for 3-4 hours or until firm to the touch.

Flip wraps and remove Paraflexx sheet. Continue to dehydrate wraps at 105° until dehydrated all the way through yet still flexible and pliable – about 5-6 more hours.

Allow to cool all the way through before storing.

Wraps can be stored in the refrigerator in a sealed container for up to one week.

spinach powder

Make your own spinach powder by dehydrating and grinding spinach in a spice grinder or purchase it from Frontier Foods – see Resources.

extra flavors

Tomato powder and nutritional yeast add great flavors to these recipes – more about them on page 22.

Mexican Wraps

Yield: about 3¼ cups of mixture or about 10-13 (6) inch wraps

BL DH

2 batches of Carrot-Ginger Juice pulp (page 34)
1 cup orange, yellow, or red bell pepper (or a combination) chopped
1 cup zucchini peeled and chopped
1 cup coconut meat
¼ cup dates pitted and finely chopped
2 Tablespoons Irish moss paste or equivalent amount of kelp noodles (see tip on page 92)
2 cups Bloomed Quinoa (page 57)
1 Tablespoon tomato powder
2 Tablespoons nutritional yeast
2½ Tablespoons Mexican Spice Blend
1¼ teaspoons salt
¼ teaspoon fresh cracked black pepper

Blend all ingredients in a high speed blender *in the order listed*, utilizing as much water as you need to blend.

Using a Paraflexx lined dehydrator tray and template (see Resources), spread a heaping ¼ cup mixture for each wrap round. Using a small offset spatula, spread the mixture flat and smooth so that it fills out the entire round evenly.

If not using template, using ¼ cup measure of mixture for each 6 inch tortilla spread evenly about ⅛ inch thick to form 4 circles for wraps on each Paraflexx sheet. Repeat until all the mixture is distributed.

Place trays in the dehydrator and dehydrate at 115° for 3-4 hours or until firm to the touch.

Flip wraps and remove Paraflexx sheet. Continue to dehydrate wraps at 105° until dehydrated all the way through yet still flexible and pliable – about 5-6 more hours.

Allow to cool all the way through before storing.

Wraps can be stored in the refrigerator in a sealed container for up to one week.

Carrot-Ginger Crackers

Tasty raw crackers can be a mainstay in any raw food home especially when weaning loved ones from the synthetic crunch factor of packaged products. We have been taught to adore crunch, and yearn for it. Here are a few easy techniques and a good basic cracker recipe that may help you bridge the gap from habit to healthy.

Yields 25-50 crackers depending on size   **NMB BL FP**

Thickener:

  1 teaspoon whole brown flax seeds
  1 teaspoon whole golden flax seeds
  2 Tablespoons water

In a small jar, combine the brown and golden flax seeds and water and soak for 4-6 hours or until thickened and gelatinous. Set aside.

Pulp:

  2½ **cups carrots** rough chopped (2 large carrots)
  3 **cups Gala apple** rough chopped (2 medium apples)
  ¼ **cup water** (optional) – use if necessary to blend

In a high speed blender place chopped carrots and apples and blend until smooth. Strain blended mixture through the **More than a Nut Milk Bag**, catching the juice in a bowl or pitcher. Reserve juice for another recipe or drink. You will be saving the pulp in the nut milk bag for use later in this recipe. Yields roughly 1 cup pulp.

recipe continues on the next page

> **pantry tip**
>
> Always have soaked and dehydrated walnuts and almonds on hand. They make great snacks or quick flours for pie crusts, bars, cookies or cakes. (see page 25 for information on soaking nuts/seeds)

1 cup walnuts soaked and dehydrated preferred but not
   necessary (see page 25)

Place walnuts in a food processor and grind to a fine meal, uniform in size, no chunks.

1 cup almond pulp

1 cup carrot-apple pulp

¼ cup ground flax meal (about 3 Tablespoons whole flax
   seeds)

1½ Tablespoons lemon juice

¼ teaspoon garlic powder

¼ teaspoon ginger powder

¼ teaspoon salt

1 Tablespoon nutritional yeast

To the food processor with the ground walnuts, add almond pulp, carrot-apple pulp, ground flax meal, lemon juice, garlic and ginger powder, salt, nutritional yeast and soaked flax seeds.

Process until mixture is well combined and uniform in consistency. Rocking the food processor helps with consistency.

Line one dehydrator tray with both grid and Paraflexx sheet. Use an off-set spatula to spread the full amount of the mixture to ⅛ - ¼ inch thick. Score into desired shapes. Note: mixture will be very thick.

Dehydrate at 115° for about 2 hours or until dry to the touch. Flip your crackers and remove the Paraflexx sheet. Continue dehydration until crackers are completely dry and crunchy – approximately 10 hours more. Crackers can be stored in an air-tight glass container for up to 3 months.

Italian Crackers &
Pizza Crust Variation

Yields: 25-35 crackers or ~10 pizza crusts   **NMB DH**

Use 1 teaspoon of the Italian Spice Blend (page 20) or make this special blend for pizza and crackers:

Pizza Seasoning Spice Blend
   ¼ **teaspoon fennel seeds**
   1 **pinch oregano**
   ⅛ **teaspoon thyme**
   ¼ **teaspoon store-bought Italian seasoning blend**

Grind all spices separately in a spice grinder or mortar and pestle and set aside. If this recipe turns out to be a hit, consider making extra Pizza Spice Blend so you always have some on hand.

Ingredients
   1 **Tablespoon olive oil**
   2 **Tablespoons tomato powder** (page 22)

Directions:

Prepare Carrot Ginger Cracker dough (page 61).

To this mixture add the pizza seasoning blend, olive oil and tomato powder and continue processing until well incorporated. You might need to stop the food processor periodically and use a spatula to scrape the sides and help incorporate ingredients into the dough uniformly. A stand mixer works beautifully to fold all ingredients together for this recipe.

recipe continues on the next page

For Italian Crackers:

Line one dehydrator tray with both grid and Paraflexx sheet. Place the mixture on the sheet and cover with a second Paraflexx sheet. Using a rolling pin, or similar, roll out the dough as best you can. Remove the top Paraflexx and continue to flatten and shape the dough using an off-set spatula to spread the full amount of the mixture to ¼ inch thick or less. Thinner is better. Score into desired shapes. Note: mixture will be very thick.

Dehydrate at 115° for about 2 hours or until dry to the touch. Flip your crackers and remove the Paraflexx sheet. Continue dehydration until crackers are completely dry and crunchy – for about another 10 hours more. Crackers can be stored in an air-tight glass container for up to 3 months.

Pizza Crust variation:

This mixture can be hand shaped into rustic mini pizza crusts.

1. Use ¼ – ½ cup of the mixture for each individual crust.

2. Roll measured amounts into balls.

3. On the solid surface or Paraflexx sheet individually knead the dough with your knuckles from the center outward, pushing up high edges to form a crust. Continue to knead and shape with your hands until you reach desired shape and thickness. Place individual crusts directly on dehydrator grid sheets – no Paraflexx needed.

4. Dehydrate at 115° for 8-9 hours until crusts are dry to the touch, yet edges are still spongy. Store in the refrigerator in an air-tight glass container for up to a week. If dried completely they can be stored in the cupboard for up to three months.

Banana Zucchini Muffins

Yield: 25-30 muffins   **NMB FP DH**

2 batches of Green Giant Juice pulp (page 35)

2 **apples** grated in food processor and squeezed through a
More than a Nut Milk Bag

2 cups **zucchini** grated in food processor and squeezed
through a ### More than a Nut Milk Bag

Place pulp, squeezed apples and squeezed zucchini in large bowl.

1 **cup dates** pitted and chopped small

1 **cup almond pulp**

4 **bananas** broken into small pieces

½ **cup chia seeds** ground in a spice grinder

½ **cup flax seeds** ground in a spice grinder

2½ **teaspoons vanilla extract**

2 **teaspoons cinnamon**

½ **teaspoon salt**

Loosely separate dates and add them to the bowl, then add the rest of these ingredients. Hand mix to incorporate all ingredients into one uniform batter.

Divide the batter into 3 or 4 equal portions. In a food processor outfitted with an 'S' blade place one portion of the batter and pulse until the batter is slightly broken down. (This helps the fresh and dried fruits, spices and flours all mix together well.) Place processed batter into another bowl. Repeat this step until all the original batter is processed.

1 **cup chopped walnuts**

Hand mix in chopped walnuts once all the mixture has been processed in food processor.

For **muffins**, use a non-stick mini-cheesecake pan or mini-muffin pan to shape. Place 3 Tablespoons of mixture into each mold. Gently remove each muffin from the pan. Transfer to a mesh screen lined dehydrator tray. Repeat until all the mixture is used.

Dehydrate initially on high, 125° for 2 hours, then drop the temperature to 115° for another 4-6 hours.

Carrot Muffins or Scones

Yield: 20-30 muffins or about 16-24 scones   **NMB FP DH**

Grate **2 apples** in food processor and squeeze them as dry as you can through a ***More than a Nut Milk Bag***. Refrigerate apple solids, and use the juice in the next step:

½ cup golden flax seeds
1½ cups water plus saved apple juice
Soak flax seeds for 8 hours.

2 batches Carrot-Ginger Juice pulp (page 34)
2 cups carrot shredded (about 4 medium carrots)

Place carrot pulp, grated squeezed apples (from the first step), and shredded carrots in a large bowl.

1 cup dates pitted and chopped small
½ cup dried apples chopped into small pieces
⅓ cup dried pineapple chopped into small pieces
2 teaspoons cinnamon
¼ teaspoon nutmeg
1 cup almond pulp
½ cup chia seeds ground in a spice grinder
½ cup flax seeds ground in a spice grinder
½ cup coconut flakes

pulp advisory

This recipe can be made from scratch or substitute 1 cup of the pulp left over from the Carrot Ginger Juice on page 34.

Loosely separate dates and add them to the bowl along with all these ingredients. Don't forget the soaked flax seeds. Hand mix to incorporate all ingredients into one uniform batter.

Divide the batter into 3 or 4 equal portions. In a food processor outfitted with an 'S' blade place one portion of the batter and pulse until the batter is slightly broken down. This helps the fresh and dried fruits, spices and flours all mix together well. Place processed batter into another bowl. Repeat this step until all the original batter is processed.

½ cup raisins
1 cup walnuts chopped

Gently hand mix in raisins and chopped walnuts once all the mixture has been processed in food processor.

For Scones: Using 2 cups of the mixture and the *Rawsome* Template as a guideline, (see resource list for ordering) shape mixture into a mound roughly the diameter of one of the template rounds. Score into 8 triangles by cutting the mound in half, then quarters, then eighths. Repeat until all of the mixture is used.

For Muffins: Use a non-stick mini-cheesecake pan or mini-muffin pan to shape. Place 3 Tablespoons of mixture into each mold. Gently remove each muffin from the pan. Transfer to a mesh screen lined dehydrator tray. Repeat until all of the mixture is used.

Dehydrate initially on high, 125° for 2 hours, then reduce the temperature to 115° for another 2-3 hours.

Garden Blend Crackers or Bread

Yield: 7 cups mixture (over 100 crackers depending on size or 25-30 mini bread "loafs" 3x3 – 1/4 inch thick)   **FP DH**

2 cloves garlic
1 cup kelp noodles

In a food processor, outfitted with an 'S' blade, place above ingredients and process until kelp noodles are broken down into tiny pieces, being sure to scrape down the sides of your vessel from time to time to help keep your mixture uniform.

2 batches of Green Giant Juice pulp (about 1½ cups of pulp – page 35)
3 cups Bloomed Quinoa (dry cup measure – page 57)
1½ cups almond pulp
½ cup chia seeds ground fine
1/4 cup nutritional yeast
1 Tablespoon Savory Seasoning Blend (page 21)
1 teaspoon thyme
⅛ teaspoon salt
1 Tablespoon olive oil
¼ cup + 2 Tablespoons Tamari

Add these ingredients to your food processing bowl and process until well incorporated, rocking the machine to help all ingredients incorporate.

Transfer your mixture from the food processor to a mixing bowl.

¾ cup zucchini shredded (about 1 medium zucchini)
¾ cup celery diced (about 3 medium celery stalks)
1 cup carrots shredded (about 1 medium carrot)
¼ cup parsley chopped
¾ cup red bell pepper diced

Hand mix these ingredients.

Divide your final mixture in half and add half your mixture back into the food processor bowl fitted with the S-blade. Pulse until the vegetables are broken down to small textured pieces throughout the mixture. Repeat this step for the remaining half of the mixture.

Return final mixture back into your mixing bowl. Using 2 cups of the mixture, sandwich between two Paraflexx sheets and use a rolling pin to flatten. Be sure to work your mixture out towards the edges of the sheets to evenly distribute.

Remove top Paraflexx sheet. Transfer flattened cracker Paraflexx sheet onto a mesh lined dehydrator tray.

For crackers: Using an offset spatula of a size that suits you, neaten up the edges until you have a uniform square. Score into crackers of your desired shape and size.

Dehydrate at 115° for 2 hours. Flip and remove Paraflexx sheet and continue to dehydrate for another 2-3 hours or until crisp.

Completely dried crackers may be stored in an airtight container in the cupboard for up to a month.

For bread: repeat steps 1-3 using 4 ½-5 cups of the mixture (depending on your thickness preference). Dehydrate at 135° for 1 hour. Flip and remove Paraflexx sheet and continue to dehydrate at this temperature for one more hour. Lower temperature to 115° and continue to dehydrate for another 5-6 hours or until bread is crisp to the touch and spongey but not doughy on the inside.

TIP: Spread the bread mixture in a large square on the tray and cut into small cubes for croutons. Dehydrate fully.

fermentation times

Fermentation times vary depending on the weather, your kitchen environment, and personal preferences. Taste your cheese often during this time to determine your personal preference and place cheese in the refrigerator once the flavor has been achieved. Refrigeration slows down the fermentation but does not stop it completely.

hot soaking and peeling almonds

To make almond cheese, the brown almond skins need to be removed from the white flesh of the almond, because leaving the skins adds an unwelcome texture and color to the cheese. The brown skin should be removed before soaking the almonds.

To remove skins:

1. Place the almonds in a medium size bowl and cover with boiling water. Let almonds soak for about 10 minutes, then drain the water and repeat. This two-step process helps to soften and begin to remove the skin without damaging the nutritional integrity of the almonds. The water does not affect the almond meat or compromise nutrition.

2. Again drain the water and pour the almonds directly on a nubby terry-cloth towel. Rub vigorously with another portion of the towel to loosen the brown outer skins. Rinse the brown bits off the peeled white almond meats and discard. Soak the white almonds for 6-8 hours in cold water. See page 44 for soaking instructions.

Cheeses

So many of us love cheese! I hear this over and over when someone thinks of "going raw": 'I could never give up cheese.' Nuts and seeds are great replacements in raw food to re-create that soft creamy cheese texture we crave. Nut cheese can be flavored and adjusted for many uses and so becomes the base for other recipes such as cheesecakes (page 91).

Almond Cheese

Yields about 2 cups   **BL NMB**

Ingredients:

1½ **cups almonds** skins removed, then soaked 6-8 hours (2 cups once soaked – see note on page 70)

⅛ **teaspoon probiotic powder OR 1 emptied capsule**

2 **cups water** to blend

Directions:

Once skins are removed and almonds are soaked 6-8 hours, rinse and drain them.

Place the white peeled almonds into a high speed blender, along with the probiotic powder and water. Blend mixture until smooth and fluffy. If necessary, use a spatula to gently guide the sides of the mixture into the center vortex, being careful not to work too deep and engage the blender blade.

Place smooth almond cheese inside a **More than a Nut Milk Bag**. Let sit in a quart jar or bowl for 2-3 hours. This allows the probiotic to incorporate into the cheese and begin the fermentation process.

Note: If you do not do this step, no worries, but allowing the mixture to rest for a couple of hours before hanging gives you a quicker, more uniform fermentation, and more of the probiotic is retained in the cheese instead of draining away.

Hang the mixture over a bowl or plate to catch any excess liquid as your cheese ferments. Leave for approximately 6-8 hours or until desired taste is achieved.

Savory Cheese

Yields about 2 cups

Ingredients:
   2 cups almond cheese
   1 Tablespoon + 1 teaspoon nutritional yeast
   1 teaspoon garlic powder
   ½ teaspoon salt
   1½ teaspoons smoked paprika
   1 teaspoon tomato powder (page 22)
   1 teaspoon maple syrup

   2 Tablespoons minced onion
   ½ cup minced bell pepper

Directions:

In a mixing bowl, fold in nutritional yeast, garlic powder, salt, paprika, tomato powder and agave. Hand mix until well-incorporated.

Once mixture is smooth and well-incorporated, add and fold in the onion and bell pepper.

nut cheese tips

✿ One **More than a Nut Milk Bag** is sufficient for the fermentation step, but two are better as this ensures you release the whey, but not too much of your cheese mixture.

✿ Over fermented cheese is not a disaster. You can flavor the cheese sweet or savory to hide the tartness if desired.

✿ If you have the smaller vessel for Vitamix or Blendtec, this is a very handy use for it.

Sweet Cheese

Yields about 2 cups

Ingredients:

  2 cups almond cheese
  2 teaspoons nutritional yeast
  1 Tablespoon + 1 teaspoon maple syrup
  ¼ cup soft apricots finely chopped
  ¼ teaspoon salt
  ¼ teaspoon vanilla extract
  ½ cup dried figs finely chopped
  1 vanilla bean, scraped (the caviar – see page 81)

Directions:

  In a mixing bowl, fold all ingredients together until well-incorporated.

---

nut cheese storage

Nut cheeses may be stored for 3-5 days, sometimes up to a week, in the refrigerator in a sealed glass container. They continue to ferment slowly so the flavor will slightly change over time. When in doubt as to the freshness of your cheese always give it the smell test. And if you see light pink coloration forming, throw it out. Remember my mantra "When in doubt, throw it out."

Cashew – Brazil Nut Cheese

Yields about 2 cups   **NMB BL**

Ingredients:
 ¾ cup cashews
 ¾ cup Brazil nuts
 ⅛ teaspoon probiotic powder OR 1 emptied capsule
 1 cup water to blend

Directions:

In a high-speed blender, blend mixture until smooth and creamy. If necessary, use a spatula to gently guide the sides of the mixture into the center vortex. Be careful not to immerse the spatula too deep into the vessel where it might get caught by the blender blade.

Place smooth Cashew – Brazil Nut Cheese inside a **More than a Nut Milk Bag**. Let sit in a quart jar or bowl for 2-3 hours. This allows the probiotic to incorporate into the cheese and begin the fermentation process.* Then hang the mixture, in a warm place, over a bowl or plate to catch any excess liquid as your cheese ferments.

Leave for approximately 6-8 hours or until desired taste is achieved. Exact time depends on location and environment.

Note: There is no need to hot soak and peel the Brazil nuts (as described in the almond cheese recipe) even though they have a brown skins. The skins are soft and break down almost completely leaving an attractive small black fleck in the cheese that does not affect the taste or texture.

* If you omit this step, no worries, but I find that allowing the mixture to set for a couple of hours before hanging gives a quicker, more uniform fermentation and better probiotic retention in the cheese.

Nacho Cheese variation

2 cups Cashew-Brazil Nut Cheese
½ cup red bell pepper chopped
2 Tablespoons lemon juice
¼ cup nutritional yeast
½ teaspoon +¼ teaspoon salt
2 large cloves of garlic
½ teaspoon turmeric
⅛ teaspoon jalapeno powder (optional)

Blend these ingredients in a high speed blender until completely incorporated.

2 teaspoons chili flakes

Pulse in chili flakes until incorporated throughout.

Cheese Nips

If you loved those cheesy little crackers, you can create a good raw version by taking this nacho cheese, spreading it thin on a Paraflexx lined dehydrator tray, scoring for small squares (the nips) and dehydrating until crispy. Once dehydrated fully they can be stored for several weeks in a glass jar in the cupboard.

---

equipment codes

At the top of each recipe, any special tools needed will be shown with the following abbreviations:

NMB – *More than a Nut Milk Bag*
BL – High Speed Blender
FP – food processor
DH – dehydrator

Parmesan Cheese

Yields about 1 cup   **NMB DH**
   1 cup Cashew – Brazil Nut Cheese
   2 Tablespoons lemon juice
   ¼ teaspoon salt
   Blend all ingredients in a high speed blender until well incorporated.

   Using a ¼ cup measuring cup, spread the mixture very thin on to Paraflexx lined dehydrator trays – ¼ cup per tray.

   Dehydrate at 115° for approximately 3-4 hours or until completely dry.

   Allow the dehydrated cheese to completely cool. Using a vegetable scraper, gently scrape the cheese into flakes and save in an air-tight container. Parmesan can be stored in the refrigerator for up to a month.

Sauces

Rich Carob Sauce

There is quite a bit of controversy about chocolate these days. 100% raw cacao is no exception. Learning your own body and how you react to certain food (fuel) is your own self discovery and it's different for *every* body. Research and personal experimentation will undoubtedly lead you to a useful conclusion about your body's tolerance for cacao – the term for the raw, 100% natural, never heated product.

My personal experience is that while my mouth and head like cacao a lot, my body's reaction is ambivalent. Cacao has a caffeine-like ingredient, theobromine, that's very stimulating.

Carob makes an acceptable substitute without the stimulant, and I have used it for years, often half and half. The combination gives me the tastes and nutritional profiles of both with a reduced bodily reaction to the cacao.

Carob is naturally sweeter than cacao and has a distinctive taste. By balancing flavors carefully, I can achieve a nice chocolatey substitute that satisfies my craving for this worldwide all-time favorite. This sauce can be used over ice cream, drizzled over cheese cake, fresh fruit (dipping strawberries?) other desserts (raw or conventional) and is a nice replacement. And again a nutritional profile with more bang for your buck.

Yields about 2½ cups   **BL**

Ingredients:
   2 cups maple syrup
   3 Tablespoons coconut oil melted (see page 78)
   1 Tablespoon olive oil
   1 teaspoon vanilla extract
   ¼ cup carob powder
   1 teaspoon lecithin

recipe continues on the next page

Directions:

Place all ingredients into a high-speed blender and blend until smooth and creamy.

Store Carob Sauce in a glass jar for up to 2 weeks in the refrigerator, or split this recipe among smaller containers and freeze for up to 3 months.

handling coconut oil

Coconut oil is a mainstay in raw cuisine. Good for you with the high omega-3 fats, solid at room temperature and with a smooth creamy consistency, it's versatile and currently plentiful worldwide. Coconut oil is solid at normal room temperatures, and more convenient to measure and use when liquefied. Here's what I do: Measure roughly twice the amount the recipe calls for and place it in a glass container in the dehydrator. The time it takes to melt depends on the amount. If you do not have a dehydrator use a warm water bath – float a small bowl with the oil inside a larger bowl with hot water. (Be sure not to get any water in the oil.)

You might be tempted to put the large coconut oil jar in the dehydrator and simply melt and pour off what you need, placing the unused portion back in your cupboard to solidify again until next needed. Don't. When the oil is heated and cooled repeatedly it oxidizes; the taste is compromised.

Raspberry Sauce

Another versatile sauce for desserts of any kind, and easy to make. Using fresh or frozen raspberries, this sauce, like the carob, freezes well and pleases almost any dessert fan.

Yields 3½ cups   **NMB BL**

Ingredients:
  3 10-oz bags frozen raspberries (about 4 cups) defrosted and drained
  1 cup golden raisins
  ½ cup maple syrup

Directions:

Place all ingredients in a high-speed blender. Blend until smooth.

Strain blended mixture through a ***More than a Nut Milk Bag*** releasing the juice and capturing the seeds to discard.

Store sauce in a glass jar for up to 1 week in the refrigerator, or split this recipe among smaller containers and freeze for up to 3 months.

Jam Variation:

Reduce the maple syrup, and you have Raspberry jam!

---

sweeten with raisins

Raisins can be used as a sweetener and thickener for a 100% whole fruit sauce. Consider, however, that dark raisins will darken the sauce, and the lovely red raspberry color will be lost. "White" or Golden raisins can be used instead, but be sure to get unsulfured raisins if any of your loved ones experience an allergic reaction to sulfur. See Resources (page 101) for our supplier, Transition Nutrition.

Marinara Sauce

This raw version of a savory all-time favorite combines chunky tomatoes, unmistakable Italian flavors of garlic, red peppers, and basil, and an added secret ingredient that make this one of my family's favorites.

Yields: 1½ cups   **NMB FP**

Ingredients:
- **3½ cups tomatoes** rough chopped (set aside 1½ cups)
- **1¼ cups rough red bell pepper** chopped (about 1 medium bell pepper)
- **1 Tablespoon tomato powder** (see page 22)
- **½ teaspoon garlic powder**
- **½ teaspoon onion powder**
- **2 Tablespoons dried basil**
- **½ teaspoon salt**
- **2 Tablespoons olive oil**
- **1 Tablespoon lemon juice**
- **½ cup rough sun-dried tomatoes** chopped (set aside)

Directions:

In a food processor outfitted with an 'S' blade add 2 cups chopped tomatoes, bell peppers, tomato powder, garlic and onion powder, basil, salt, olive oil and lemon juice. Process until smooth.

Add the sun-dried tomatoes to the food processor and pulse until well incorporated, but still slightly chunky.

Add the 1½ cups chopped tomatoes you set aside and pulse briefly until well incorporated, but still chunky.

Place mixture in a ***More than a Nut Milk Bag*** and suspend above a bowl or plate to catch excess liquid. (Drink this wonderfully seasoned tomato juice or save for inclusion in a dressing or sauce recipe.)

Remove after 1-2 hours. Mixture should be thick and chunky.

Caramel Sauce

Yield: 1½ - 2 cups   **BL**

Ingredients:
   1 teaspoon vanilla extract
   ½ teaspoon salt
   ¾ cup zucchini peeled and chopped
   ¼ cup + 2 Tablespoons agave nectar (⅜ cup)
   ½ cup date paste
   ½ cup coconut oil melted

Directions:
   In a high-speed blender place all ingredients and blend until smooth.

   Will keep in the refrigerator in a glass jar for about a week.

---

real vanilla instead

For more authentic taste or to eliminate the alcohol carrier in the vanilla extract, use vanilla beans. Carefully slice through one side of the bean lengthwise. Using a spoon or the back of your knife, scrape the moist seeds and pith from the inside of the vanilla bean. This is where most of the flavor is. Adjust the amount of liquid to compensate for the absent extract and for the different flavor intensity of the raw product. After processing, strain the sauce through a **More than a Nut Milk Bag** to remove any remaining pulp from the vanilla bean.

Almond Butter Crunch Cookies

So many love Peanut Butter cookies and I'm no different. Here's my almond butter version with an introduction to one of my go-to ingredients, *buckwheaties* – buckwheat groats (the base portion of the buckwheat before any sort of cutting, slicing, roasting etc.) soaked and dehydrated to crispy. I keep them in my cupboard in case I need to add a crunch factor on ice cream, fruit parfaits, or for an easy morning cereal without added sweetness. Some mornings I just want a bowl of buckwheaties, fresh blueberries, almond milk – I'm good to go. Buckwheat groats come hulled and un-hulled. The hulled version is used in this recipe. These cookies don't last long around my house, and they will freeze if you want to double or even triple the recipe.

Yields about 40 cookies   **DH FP**

Ingredients:
   2 cups buckwheaties (buckwheat groats, soaked and
      dehydrated) set aside
   1½ cups almond flour
   1 cup almond pulp
   ½ cup palm sugar powdered
   2 teaspoons salt

   ¾ cup almond butter
   1½ teaspoons vanilla extract
   3 Tablespoons sesame oil
   2 Tablespoons coconut oil melted

Directions:
   In a food processor add the dry ingredients; almond flour and pulp, palm sugar and salt. Process lightly until a uniform flour mixture is achieved.
   To the flour mixture in the food processor add the almond

butter, vanilla, sesame and coconut oils and continue to process until well incorporated.

Set the mixture aside in a medium size bowl and fold in the buckwheat groats completely.

For Cookies: Form dough into small balls, approximately 1 tablespoon each, and press flat with fork or the palm of your hand, onto Paraflexx sheets or something similar. This allows you to shape cookies flat without leaving a grid pattern from the grid sheet which you will use to dehydrate on.

Remove cookies from the Paraflexx and place directly on dehydrator grid sheets and dehydrate at 105°-115° for 4-5 hours or until desired consistency is achieved.

For Bars: Press dough into a square ovenproof pan lined with parchment paper, cut into bars and refrigerate for at least 2 hours, or dehydrate. The parchment paper allows for easy removal of the 'dough' once set.

Cookies or Bars will keep in the refrigerator for up to one week or may be frozen for up to 3 months.

coconut palm sugar

There are many different palm sugars on the market. As a granulated sweetener they can be used interchangeably. I prefer coconut palm sugar because it's easier on the digestion than other more popular sugar substitutes. Seek a minimally processed product from a packager you trust. The brown color means the natural sugars are intact. In this recipe I suggest 'powdering' the palm sugar, a useful technique for quick dispersion and consistent flavoring. You can skip this step, but putting the sugar in a spice or coffee grinder achieves a smoother consistency. Remove any large chunks of sugar, common in the packaged palm sugars.

Easy Seed Energy Bars

I'm always wanting something quick and easy fuel for my on-the-go days in the car or travel time away from home, and these quick easy nutrient-dense seed bars are just the thing. Sprouting the seeds adds additional nutritional value to an already packed winning combination. Seeds are concentrated foods full of good fats, vital minerals, omega 3's, protein, fiber and EFAs (essential fatty acids). As with all dehydrated foods, always be sure to consume enough water so your body doesn't need to steal precious fluids to re-hydrate this fast-start nutrition.

Yield: 6½ cups of mixture or about 25 bars   **NMB DH**
   1½ **cups sesame seeds**
   1 **cup pumpkin seeds**
   1 **cup sunflower seeds**
   4 **cups water**

Place the sesame, pumpkin and sunflower seeds in a jar, cover with water and set aside. Allow to soak for 3-4 hours.

In a separate jar place the following ingredients:
   ¼ **cup golden flax seeds**
   ½ **cup water**

Gently stir or shake your jar to allow seeds and water to incorporate and soak for 3-4 hours.

Drain the soaked sesame, pumpkin and sunflower seeds through a ***More than a Nut Milk Bag*** and rinse thoroughly. Place in a medium sized mixing bowl and set aside.

Add to your mixing bowl:
   1 **cup almond pulp** (page 45)
   ¼ **cup chia seeds** powdered in a spice grinder
   ¼ **teaspoon salt**
   1 **cup dried cranberries**
   ½ **cup raisins**
   ½ **cup cashews** roughly chopped

Gently mix all ingredients together until well incorporated. Then add to the mixing bowl:

Soaked flax seeds

¾ cup maple syrup

¼ cup sesame oil

1 Tablespoon toasted sesame oil

Using a rubber spatula fold in the soaked flax seeds, maple syrup, sesame oil and toasted sesame oil until well incorporated.

Using a 1 cup measure, measuring out 3¼ cups of mixture onto a dehydrator tray lined with Paraflexx sheet. Spread evenly into a ¼ inch thick square, and score into desired size bars.

Repeat this process for the remaining mixture.

Dehydrate at 115° for 4 hours. Flip bars using a second dehydrator tray and remove the Paraflexx sheet. Dehydrate for another 15-20 hours or until desired texture is achieved.

Allow to cool completely before storing. Store in an airtight container for up to six months.

Energy Bars

Here's a second option for those on the go quick energy bites. Utilizing the crunch from the Almond Butter Crunch Cookie recipe (page 82) this cookie morphs into a moist tasty bar or nugget to keep you going around town, in the airports or on a hike. Versatile and easy. Substitute other dried fruits, seeds or nuts for your own version.

Yields 15-20 2x1 inch Bars   **NMB**

Ingredients:

1 batch Almond Butter Crunch Cookies before dehydration (from recipe on page 82)

4½ cups shredded sweet apple (about 3 medium apples)

recipe continues on the next page

Strain shredded apples through a **_More than a Nut Milk Bag_**, releasing as much juice as possible.

3 Tablespoons cacao nibs
½ cup dried cherries chopped
½ cup cashews chopped
¼ cup pumpkin seeds
¾ cup raisins
1 cup Medjool dates chopped small (about 8-9 large)
    Add all ingredients listed above to the apples and pre-made Almond Butter Crunch Cookie mixture in a medium size bowl.

Gently knead and fold all ingredients into this mixture until well incorporated.

Press mixture into an 8x8 inch glass ovenproof pan, and place in the refrigerator or freezer until set (about 4-5 hours in the refrigerator; about an hour in the freezer).

¼ cup hemp seeds (garnish; optional)
    After mixture has set, cut into bars (2x1x1) or nuggets (1" square) and remove from pan. Roll individually in hemp seeds if desired.

Store between parchment paper in an airtight class container. Energy bars can be stored in the freezer for up to three months or the refrigerator for one week.

Variation:
Energy bars or nuggets can be dehydrated by placing them on dehydrator trays (no Paraflexx sheets needed). Dehydrate for 12-24 hours or until desired consistency is reached.

Shortbread

I'm always looking at classic recipes and creatively converting them to my new healthier raw food lifestyle. Traditional shortbread cookies have loads of flour, butter, sugar and vanilla. I thought, hmm, I can do that **healthier!** So here's my raw version of shortbread cookies with a variation, one of my favorites, Lemon Bars. I think you'll enjoy them both and the lemony tang in the bar icing is *soooo* good.

Yields 2½ cups or about 24 cookies   **FP**

8"x8" square spring-form pan

- 1 cup macadamia nuts
- 1 cup cashews
- 1 cup coconut flour
- 1 teaspoon salt

Place into a food processor outfitted with an 'S' blade and process into a fine meal.

Add:

- ½ cup almond pulp
- ½ cup agave nectar
- 2 teaspoons vanilla extract
- 2 Tablespoons coconut oil melted (see page 78 for handling tips)
- 2 teaspoons flax oil

> **coconut flour**
>
> Coconut flour can easily be made by grinding coconut flakes in a spice or coffee grinder.

Continue processing until well incorporated. Press finished shortbread mixture into a parchment lined square 8x8-inch spring-form pan, and allow to set-up in the refrigerator until firm to the touch (about 3-5 hours).

Cut into desired cookie shapes and serve. Shortbread Cookies will keep in the refrigerator stored in a sealed glass container for up to one week and the freezer for up to 3 months.

Lemon Bars

Yields about 24 lemon bars

1 batch shortbread pressed into 8"x8" square spring-form pan; set aside

2 cups golden raisins

1 cup lemon juice (enough to cover raisins)

Place raisins and lemon juice in a bowl or container and allow to soak 3-5 hours.

¼ cup + 2 Tablespoons clear agave nectar

⅜ teaspoon turmeric

2 Tablespoons coconut oil melted (see page 78 for handling tips)

Place agave nectar, turmeric, and coconut oil, along with golden raisins and lemon juice into a high-speed blender, and blend until mixture is smooth.

Pour blended mixture on top of pressed shortbread in the spring-form pan.

Allow to set-up in the refrigerator overnight and cut into desired shapes for Lemon Bars before serving. Lemon Bars will keep in the refrigerator stored in a sealed glass container for up to 1 week or in the freezer for up to 3 months

Note: Lemon Bar topping can be stored in bulk in the refrigerator or freezer. Consider making the shortbread cookies and freezing, saving the lemon bar topping to add before serving.

Spiced Biscotti

I've loved biscotti for as long as I can remember. In the morning with a cup of tea or for afternoon snack this traditional Italian cookie is enjoyed by many. The name means *twice cooked*, so this version is fundamentally different because in raw cuisine we don't cook. Are we really making biscotti? For purists, probably not, but for me and countless others looking for a gluten-free snack *like* biscotti, this one is a winner.

Yield: 30-40 biscotti depending on thickness   **DH**

Dry Ingredients:
- 2 cups almond pulp
- 1 cup almond flour
- ¼ cup palm sugar, powdered (see tip page 83)
- 1 teaspoon ginger
- ⅛ teaspoon cardamom
- 1 pinch orange zest
- ¼ teaspoon salt

Wet Ingredients:
- 1 cup soft Medjool dates chopped (about 8 large dates)
- 1 Tablespoon vanilla extract
- 3⅛ Tablespoons coconut oil melted (see page 78 for handling tips)

recipe continues on the next page

interchangeable sugars

Palm and Date sugar are interchangeable in recipes calling for a sugar with dry granular consistency. These sugars can usually be found on the bakery row of natural food stores or co-ops.

the "perfect bite"

Remember the "perfect bite" (page 12) and chop the dates, apricots, and pistachios the same small sizes as they will be hand mixed into your biscotti dough.

Directions

In a medium size bowl hand mix dry ingredients together. Add the dates, vanilla and coconut oil and hand mix until well incorporated.

¼ cup apricots finely chopped (about 3-4)

½ cup pistachios rough chopped

Gently knead in chopped apricots and pistachios.

On a cookie sheet or something similar, shape entire dough mixture into a loaf and place in freezer overnight.

Thinly slice the loaf into individual biscotti cookies and place separately on dehydrator trays with grid sheets – no Paraflexx needed.

Dehydrate at 115° for 24 -36 hours.

equipment codes

At the top of each recipe, any special tools needed will be shown with the following abbreviations:

NMB – *More than a Nut Milk Bag*

BL – High Speed Blender

FP – food processor

DH – dehydrator

Cheesecakes

Who wants Cheesecake? I know, everyone always seems to want desserts and cheesecake is at the top of the list. Raw versions of this classic can be too 'nut heavy' for my taste so I've tried to lighten things up a bit (with the addition of coconut meat and Irish moss or kelp noodles) while keeping the creaminess and texture we all love in a good New York style cake. Adding fermented almond cheese gets closer to that original New York texture and taste but if you don't have time to ferment the cheese, make this recipe anyway. It'll still be great and your guests will be coming back for more.

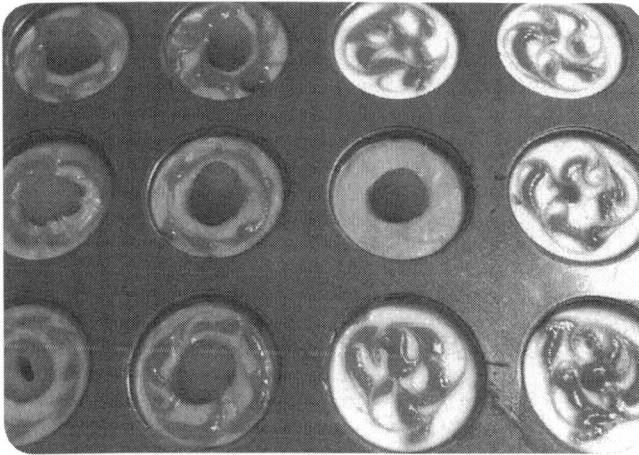

individual cheesecakes

Meagan makes the cutest little single-serving cheesecakes! Use standard muffin tins and cupcake papers, or smaller mini-cheesecake pans available at culinary stores. Divide the crust and filling so each mini-cake is pleasingly full. You can freeze these little treasures and pop them out when you need a sweet snack or a little something to top off a meal.

Vanilla Cheesecake

Yields 9-inch cake (12-16 servings)

BL FP 8x8 inch spring-form pan

Crust: *yields 1½ cups*

- **1 cup almond pulp**
- **½ cup coconut flour**
- **2 Tablespoons coconut palm sugar** powdered
- **2 Tablespoons carob powder** (raw not toasted – see page 77)
- **¼ teaspoon salt**

Place all ingredients into a food processor outfitted with an 'S' blade and process until well incorporated.

Add to vessel:

- **½ cup dates** chopped and pitted
- **½ teaspoon vanilla extract**

Continue processing until well incorporated.

Press final crust mixture into a parchment-lined 8x8 inch spring-form pan. Set aside.

Irish moss & kelp noodles

Many raw food dessert recipes call for Irish Moss Paste. This is a wonderful binder for our desserts and a healthy ingredient too – it's seaweed. Instead of making the paste you can achieve the same texture and binding quality in raw desserts by blending the cleaned and soaked Irish Moss with your other ingredients. Alternatively, Kelp Noodles may be substituted in equivalent measure and in the same way if Irish moss is hard to find. Kelp Noodles are more widely available at the market – ask your grocer to stock them.

To clean Irish Moss or Kelp Noodles: Rinse under running water, pick out any sand or dirt, and remove any dark pieces. Add enough clean water to cover and soak for 2-3 hours – until soft to the touch and expanded – not hard and brittle. Rinse several times before use.

Filling: *yields about 3½ cups*

¾ cup coconut meat

1 cup almond cheese

2½ Tablespoons Irish moss rinsed and soaked packed
measure, or rinsed and soaked kelp noodles. (See tip on
page 92.) Cut into small bits with culinary scissors

1½ teaspoons vanilla extract

¼ cup + 2 Tablespoons clear agave nectar

¼ cup Cashew-Brazil-Hempseed Milk (page 47)

2 Tablespoons lemon juice

¼ teaspoon salt

Place coconut meat, almond cheese, Irish moss (or kelp
noodles), vanilla, agave, nut milk, lemon juice and salt into a
high-speed blender. Blend on high until completely smooth
and incorporated.

Add to the blender vessel:

1 Tablespoon soy lecithin powder (see below)

2 Tablespoons coconut oil melted

Blend on high until completely smooth and incorporated.

Pour blended filling on top of pressed crust. Spread top
smooth using a small off-set spatula.

Allow to set up in the refrigerator overnight or until knife
cuts firm and cleanly all the way through. (Overnight is best.)

Cheesecake will store in the refrigerator for up to one week
and frozen up to 3 months.

---

soy lecithin

Be sure to get a GMO free soy lecithin when adding this ingredient to your raw food kitchen. Available
at health foods stores it is shelf stable for months. For
those who avoid soy there is a sunflower lecithin on the
market. My experience is only with a liquid version of
sunflower lecithin so it would not be an equivalent measure or texture as a direct replacement in this recipe.

Raspberry Cheesecake

Yields 8x8 inch cake or 12-16 servings **BL**
    Crust Yield – 1½ cups
    Filling Yield – about 3½ cups

Crust:

1 batch Vanilla Cheesecake Crust Recipe (page 92)

Press final crust mixture into a parchment lined 8x8-inch spring-form pan. Set aside.

Filling:

1 batch Vanilla Cheesecake Filling Recipe (page 93)
¾ cup Raspberry Sauce Recipe (page 79)

Place all ingredients into a high-speed blender. Blend on high until completely smooth and incorporated.

Pour blended filling into pressed crust. Spread top smooth using a small off-set spatula.

Allow to set up in the refrigerator overnight or until knife cuts firm and clean all the way through. Garnish with raspberries if desired.

Chocolate Cheesecake

Yields 8x8 inch cake or 12-16 servings   **BL**
   Crust Yield – 1½ cups
   Filling Yield – about 3½ cups

Crust:

1 batch Vanilla Cheesecake Crust Recipe (page 92)

Press final crust mixture into a parchment lined 8x8-inch spring-form pan. Set aside.

Filling:

1 batch Vanilla Cheesecake Filling Recipe (page 93)
1½ Tablespoons carob powder
3 Tablespoons raw cacao powder
2 Tablespoons maple syrup
¾ teaspoon salt

Place all ingredients into a high-speed blender. Blend on high until completely smooth and incorporated.

Pour blended filling into crust. Spread top smooth using a small off-set spatula.

Allow to set up in the refrigerator overnight or until knife cuts firm and clean all the way through.

"raw" cacao

Some raw cacao on the market is not truly raw so the 'know your source' caveat always comes into play. Do some research, pay attention to how you feel after consuming cacao, like you would anything on your healthy food journey and decide for yourself.

Ice Cream

Everyone's favorite. The raw version can be creamy and luscious enough to satisfy cravings for the good old days of hand cranks and ice cream parties in the back yard. I grew up with ice cream socials and we kids were always enlisted to turn the cranks of the old hand versions of what nowadays is a kitchen electric gadget worth having.

Maple Vanilla Ice Cream

Yields: 5½ cups   **BL**

Ingredients:
   2 cups thick coconut meat
   2 cups Cashew-Brazil-Hempseed Milk (page 47)
   1½ cups maple syrup
   2 Tablespoons + 1 teaspoon vanilla extract
   ½ teaspoon salt
   2 Tablespoons soy lecithin powder
   2 Tablespoons coconut oil melted
   2 vanilla beans scraped (see page 81)

Directions:
   Place all ingredients into a high speed blender vessel, and blend on high until smooth, approximately 1 minute. Place in shallow sealed glass container and place in freezer until set – overnight is best.

   Will keep in freezer for up to 3 months.

---

ice cream freezer

An electric ice cream freezer may be used for these recipes but it's not necessary. After processing, store in a shallow glass container overnight to set firm. If using an ice cream freezer, you will still store the mixture in a glass container in the freezer.

Strawberry Ice Cream

Yields 8 cups   **BL**

1 Maple Vanilla Ice Cream recipe (before freezing)
2 cups strawberries defrosted and drained (about 2
    10-ounce bags) – catch and reserve the juice for sauce.
    Note: 1½ cups fresh strawberries may be substituted;
    chop into small pieces.

Place all ingredients into a high speed blender vessel, and
blend on high until smooth, approximately 1 minute, or until
smooth. Place in sealed glass container and place in freezer
until set – overnight is best.

Will keep in freezer for up to 3 months

Chocolate Ice Cream

Yields 6 cups   **BL**

1 Maple Vanilla Ice Cream recipe (before freezing)
¼ cup + 2 Tablespoons cacao powder
¼ teaspoon salt

Place all ingredients into a high speed blender vessel, and
blend on high until smooth, approximately 1 minute, or until
smooth. Place in shallow sealed glass container and place in
freezer until set – overnight is best.

Will keep in freezer for up to 3 months.

---

equipment codes

At the top of each recipe, any special tools needed
will be shown with the following abbreviations:

NMB – *More than a Nut Milk Bag*
BL – High Speed Blender
FP – food processor
DH – dehydrator

---

metrics

⅛ teaspoon .... .5 ml
¼ teaspoon .... 1 ml
½ teaspoon ....2.5 ml
1 teaspoon .... 5 ml
1 Tablespoon .... 3 teaspoons ....15 ml
4 Tablespoons .... ¼ cup ....59 ml
                          ⅓ cup............. 79 ml
                          ½ cup...........118 ml
                          1 cup ....237 ml

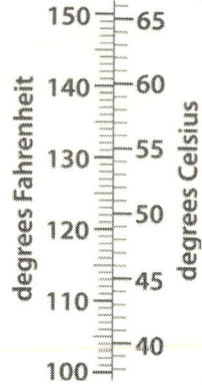

degrees Fahrenheit

150
140
130
120
110
100

degrees Celsius

65
60
55
50
45
40

More than a Nut Milk Bag Recipe Collection

Glossary

Following are some of the terms and ingredients used in the recipes in this collection. I kept the recipes simple and with ingredients that can usually be found at your local health or natural foods store. I include a couple of my favorite special ingredients; certainly, substitutions can be made as you begin to understand more about the five flavors and what they represent.

Agave Nectar – A natural sweetener made from the agave plant. Lower on the glycemic index than honey or maple syrup, it is not a raw product.

Blender – high speed blenders such as the Vitamix and Blendtec offer blending capabilities of 2½ to 3 horsepower and blend soups, smoothies, sauces and nut milks in seconds.

Cacao – natural 100% raw chocolate from a cacao pod is available in powder, nibs or paste. It contains a caffeine analog, theobromine, that some find over-stimulating. The health benefits of cacao are controversial so I invite you to discover for yourself how your body reacts to cacao.

Carob – this dark brown powder, made from carob seeds and pods, is often used as a chocolate substitute. It is free of caffeine. Available raw or toasted; I prefer raw.

Dehydrator – warms and dries food at low temperatures. Use for "cooking" foods without compromising the nutrient content. The most well known and effective is made by Excalibur and I recommend the 9 tray with Paraflexx sheets.

enzyme inhibitors – naturally occurring chemicals, often found on the husks or skins of seeds, that discourage insects and bacteria from eating the seeds. These compounds are often bitter and even mildly poisonous.

Green Tea – There is no such thing as fine green tea in tea bags. As with good knives, with good tea you get what you pay for, and the cheap stuff is usually a bitter, oxidized powder – sweepings from the tea factory floor. If you're trying to reduce your caffeine intake, treat yourself to the priciest loose green tea you can find. Use good green tea sparingly, and more than once. The best leaves are said to make their best tea on the second and third brewings.

Himalayan Salt – considered the purest salt on the planet, it is uncontaminated by any toxins or pollutants as it's mined high in the Himalayan mountains, an area of the earth not touched by civilization's pollutants. Highly beneficial to overall health.

julienne cut – long skinny bits, like shoestring potatoes.

Miso – a white, yellow, or red paste usually made from fermented soybeans. There are non-soy versions available.

packed measure – pack ingredient into measure tightly.

Nut Milk Bag – a nylon mesh bag used for many things including straining nut milks, juices, and sauces to separate the pulp from the liquid. We are especially proud of our own *More than a Nut Milk Bags*. Buy them online at *RawsomeCreations.com*

Rough chop – uniform sized pieces not necessarily the same shape. This method is usually used when ingredients are to be blended so there is no need for exact sizes or shapes.

Young Thai Coconuts – the meat and water from these coconuts are a wonderful source of electrolytes, calcium, purified water and saturated fat. Coconut water is very similar to human blood plasma and extremely beneficial.

Resources

For a handy list of links for these and other useful resources, you are invited to visit this book's online website at **rawsomecreations.com/rcreader**

Environmental Working Group website : ewg.org

CSA – Community Supported Agriculture – an arrangement between farmers and their customer that helps finance the former while securing a reliable supply of healthy food. Often CSA members pre-pay, thereby providing funds to the farmer for seeds and amendments. In return, members usually get a weekly box full of delicious produce. Find a CSA near you at localharvest.org

Buck Mountain Maple Syrup Farm in northern Vermont. Good friends Gwyneth, Matt and Galadriel tap their 5,000+ sugar maples each year to provide us loyal fans with wonderful family grown organic Vermont maple and I love it! On the web at buckmountainmaple.com

TransitionNutrition.com offers unsulfured golden Himalayan raisins, Himalayan salt, and a variety of coconut products.

frontiercoop.com – source for spinach powder and other flavor enhancers

alongerhealthylife.com and Raw Food Chefs Diane Haworth and Michael Varbaek for inspiration and food ideas.

food grade acrylic TEMPLATE from RawsomeCreations.com helps users make perfectly round wraps and tortillas.

Invitation

This is a "living book" in the sense that my discoveries never stop. You are invited to join my free monthly newsletter with new **More than a Nut Milk Bag** ideas, tools of the trade, and raw food news. My website,

rawsomecreations.com

is also full of information and links to more about raw food, including an online version of these Resources with links that actually work – much better than a book.

As an owner of this book, you are entitled to visit the special, ever growing library of Nut MIlk Bag tips and tricks that may be found at

rawsomecreations.com/rcreader
Your username is **rawsome**
and your password is **morethan**
note: all addresses, username, and password are **lower case**

Index

P

palm sugar 82, 83, 92
pantry tip 61
paprika, smoked 72
paraflexx 14
Parmesan Cheese 76
parsley 35, 36, 42, 68
parsnips 29
peas 51
peeling
  almonds 70
  citrus 30
  fruits and veggies 30
pepper, bell 60, 68, 72, 75, 80
perfect bite, the 12
phytonutrients 26, 39, 40, 42, 46
pinch 50
pineapple, dried 66
pistachios 90
Pizza Crust 63, 64
Pizza Seasoning Spice Blend 63
potassium 39, 45
powder
  cacao 95, 97
  carob 77, 95
  garlic 58, 80
  jalapeno 75
  mushroom 22
  onion 51, 58, 80
  probiotic 71
  soy lecithin 93
  spinach 22, 58
  tomato 22, 80
pre-soaking 44
probiotic powder 71, 74
prostate cancer 40
psyllium powder 53, 55
pulp 31
  almond 62, 65, 66, 68, 82, 87,
    89, 92
  carrot-apple 62
  Carrot-Ginger Juice 60, 66
  Green Giant Juice 58, 65
pumpkin seeds 86
pungent (taste) 23

Q

quinoa, bloomed 56, 57, 58, 60, 68

R

raisins 86
  golden 79, 88
raspberries 79
Raspberry Cheesecake 94
Raspberry Sauce 79
Raw Food Chef Instructor 9
raw living foods 26
Rawsome Creations 112
real vanilla instead 81
recipe format 11
recycling 24
resveratrol 39, 42
Rich Carob Sauce 77
rough chop 29, 100

S

salt 19
salty (taste) 23
Sauces 77
Savory Cheese 72
Savory Seasoning Blend 21, 68
Scones, Carrot 66
scoring 27
scraps 24
seedless grapes 38
seeds and stems 31
selenium 47
Shortbread 87
skins, fruit and vegetable 30
slow oven 26
smidgen 50
snow peas 50
soaking
  nuts 25
  seeds 25
Soup 48
  skills 48
sour (acid - taste) 23
soy lecithin 93
spice blends 19
Spiced Biscotti 89

How to clean your
More than a Nut Milk Bag:

Empty nut, veggie or fruit pulp into another bag or container and wash the bag completely under running warm water. Hang to air dry. For stubborn stains, soak the bag in GSE (grapefruit seed extract) and water.

Testimonials:

I just received my nut milk bags. Best creation ever!!!!

– D Lerner

Received the nut milk bags and I just love them. They are so easy to use, sturdy, convenient and great to purchase something you need that makes a difference. The young son of a client of mine likes to "milk" the bag while we are making cashew milk for him.

– Raw Food Consultant

Thank you for offering this quality product on your website!

I'll let you know when I come up with other uses for the bags…herbal infusions for sure.

– Cathy Vogt
anaturalchef.com

People just love your nut milk bags by the way! They work so great.

– Lee Anne
Truly Organics, trulyorganicfoods.com

Thank you so much for the milk bag!! :) I have made a green juice with it almost every morning with the blender and also a lot of almond milk :) You're awesome!

– Jessica King

Loving my bag! Better than the other one I have :-)

– Kai Brava

The milk goes through so fast and strains really well...

–anonymous fan

The More than a NUT MILK BAG Story

I started my love affair with Bali long before we met in person, and each time I return, she rises to meet me with a soft welcoming spirit I feel in no other place. My time in Bali is filled with magic moments, every step of the way. Each time, I find myself awed by her people: their open-hearted way of living, their reverence for spirit and nature, and their overwhelming sense of belonging to something grander than their everyday world.

I've made some amazing friends through the years, two of whom are doing incredible work for the children of Bali. My **More than a Nut Milk Bag** project began with a simple idea to create work opportunities for local women while generating much needed funding for some worthy causes.

Each year I visit, I go to see the seamstress who makes my wonderful bags. She puts so much love into each one, I can feel it when I unpack them back home. I'm so happy to be able to bring this little piece of Bali to my friends back in the US. So when you consider buying my **More than a Nut Milk Bags**, please remember that this little exercise of the Fair Trade principle helps support the seamstress and also helps two charities which are near and dear to me.

Bumi Sehat Birthing Center
(bumisehatbali.org) is a a world-renowned mother and child welfare project founded by Ibu Robin Lim. (Ibu is an honorary title that means "Mother.") Bumi Schat is a non-profit, village-based organization of dedicated families, midwives, doctors, nurses, teachers and volunteers from Indonesia and around the world.

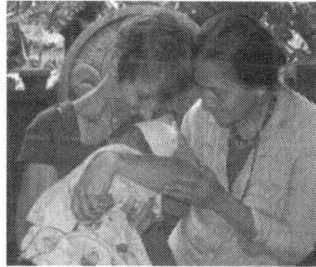

Yayasan Widya Guna Orphanage is near Ubud, Bali. Being parentless in a developing country is hard enough; imagine being parentless and handicapped! (You can't.) Yayasan Widya Guna Orphanage is one of the only resources for handicapped children on the island.

Both of these charities are independently funded by donations from around the world. A portion of every purchase of a **More than a Nut Milk Bag** goes to these very worthy charities.

More than a Nut Milk Bag

A versatile multi-tasker for your kitchen

✳ FAIR TRADE – made in Bali, Indonesia by Wayan and her friends

✳ 100% nylon – sanitary, stain-resistant, easy to clean – 10x12 inches – 2.5+ Quart capacity

✳ Fine mesh minimizes sediment and allows for sprouting of even the smallest of seeds and grains

✳ Bias cut and serge-stitched seams ensure flexibility and durability

✳ Multi-tasker, Multiple uses, Reusable – Easy to place over a pitcher for straining – Great for Travel

✳ Seams on the outside help keep the bag clean – thoroughly tested in production environment

✳ Re-usable bag for storage – Recipes and instructions on label

✳ This nut milk bag is reusable. It can be used for nut milks and straining juices. It's so much easier and faster than using a strainer. The drawstring means you can just hang it and let it do its own thing!

a note about nylon

After testing bags constructed with natural fibers, we found that nylon, over time, is the only satisfactory material. Nylon, being non-porous, makes our bags easy to clean after use, so the bags stay clean and remain strong and intact for many, many uses. We found that natural fiber bags stain quickly and tend to add unwelcome smells and tastes to their contents after only a few uses, but nylon remains neutral.

So many uses, so little time!

Nut and seed milk – Soak nuts or seeds desired time, blend with water. To strain pulp from liquid, pour mixture into the bag and put light pressure on the bag from the bottom to squeeze the milk out. Pulp can be frozen to save for other recipes such as cookies, pie crust, breads, cakes or biscotti. ***See page 43***

Fruit Sauce – Blend fruit and strain through bag following the above directions. You can drink the fruit juice, freeze it for ice pops, add it to your favorite smoothie or use to decorate a decadent dessert. ***page 79***

Sprouting – Soak sprouting seeds for desired time and hang to dry in the bag. Water twice daily until short tails appear and the seeds are sprouted. Great for sprouting while travelling so tuck it in your suitcase and you're good to go.

Juicing – Blend fresh vegetables and or greens with a bit of water and strain the mixture through the bag. Save the pulp for crackers or soups and drink the juice immediately for the greatest nutritional value. ***See page 33***

Teas – Place loose tea in bag and lower into warm water to steep. Removing after desired time and returning the leaves to Mother Earth for amazing compost. ***See page 40***

Cheese – Follow your favorite recipe for raw food nut or seed cheeses. After blending, place the cheese mixture in the bag to ferment and hang above a bowl to catch the whey. Once fermented mix in herbs and spices and enjoy! ***See page 71***

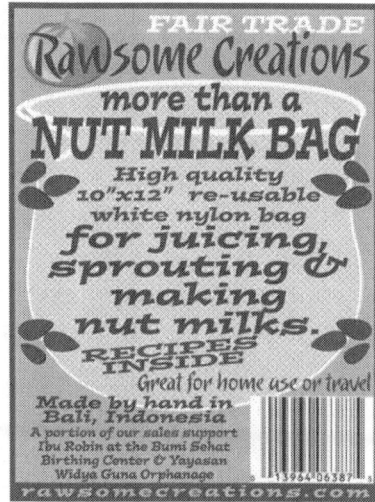

FAIR TRADE

Rawsome Creations

more than a
NUT MILK BAG

High quality
10"x12" re-usable
white nylon bag
*for juicing,
sprouting &
making
nut milks.*
**RECIPES
INSIDE**
Great for home use or travel

Made by hand in
Bali, Indonesia
A portion of our sales support
Ibu Robin at the Bumi Sehat
Birthing Center & Yayasan
Widya Guna Orphanage

rawsomecreations.com

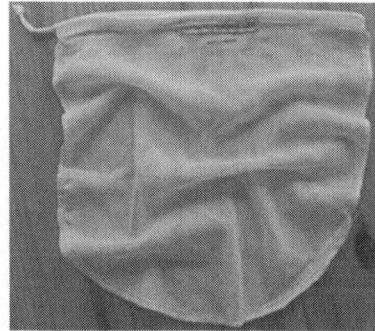

111

Chef Brenda

Brenda Hinton has been a part of the holistic lifestyle movement for many years, working with subtle energies.

Through the years, seeing the success of animal clients when their diets were adjusted to include more raw food components, she continued refining her own diet to include more plant-based options. She began an in-depth study of the diet / disease connection when diagnosed with breast cancer. Today, cancer free, she remains committed to her passion, through personal experience, that we are indeed what we eat and In addition, we are a product of our environment. Both of these things can be changed to affect our healing at the most basic level.

As a raw food enthusiast and Raw Food Chef and Instructor, Brenda's strong desire is to get to the bottom of our health stories and assist clients in changing from the inside out.

Rawsome Creations, her newest endeavor, was created as a way for her to assist people new to raw food, transitioning from a SAD (Standard American Diet), or are interested in health, healing and the diet/disease connection. Her intention is to teach through demonstrations, lectures, and consultations and to share her gastronomical raw creations with as many people as possible.

Brenda is continually refining her craft. Always researching, evaluating, and offering the latest in healing therapies to her clients, she consults in person or by telephone anywhere in the world.

In addition to being a "foodie" Brenda is a recreational runner looking forward to her fourth half-marathon. She lives in a solar home in Northern California with her husband.

13716706R00065